With affection,

Guy Baer

We move from one relationship to the next, expecting that each will make us happy. Or we stay in relationships, trying to change our partners and hoping they'll give us what we want. And most of us are afraid, angry, alone, and unhappy only because we don't know what to do.

We can change the way we live.

In *The Truth About Relationship*s, everyone can learn how to bring Real Love into their relationships and unlimited happiness into their lives.

"This book is head and shoulders above anything out there about relationships. It touched me... I could not wait to turn each page. It was like stepping from the shadows into the sun! Dr. Baer has given us a monumental achievement in understanding Real Love and relationships."
-Richard Fuller, Metaphysical Reviews

"*The Truth About Relationships* is an awesome and essential contribution to the understanding of love and relationships. It's an intimate and truthful work of art, a modern masterpiece. Move over, John Gray! Greg Baer is the ultimate relationship expert."
-Matthew Grey and Angelina, Love Life Radio Globalcast

"Dr. Baer's insight and common sense are astonishing. He exposes relationships for what they are with a quiver full of arrows that hit on-target. This sensitive and vivid book destroys the barriers to love in any relationship."
-The Book Reader

The
Truth About
Relationships

Second Edition

A Simple and Powerfully Effective Way
For Everyone to Find
Real Love and Loving Relationships

Greg Baer, M.D.

Baer, Greg
      The Truth About Relationships
      Includes index
      ISBN 1-892319-07-1
      1. Relationships 2. Self Help 3. Psychology/Psychiatry

Library of Congress Catalog Number: 00-191398

Second Edition: January, 2001

Published by:

Blue Ridge Press
P.O. Box 3075
Rome, GA 30164
(706) 234-9745

Also by
Greg Baer, M.D.

The Wart King, The Truth About Love and Lies
The Wise Man, Telling the Truth and Finding Love
The Truth About Parenting

Printed in the United States of America

10 9 8 7 6 5 4 3 2 1

Acknowledgements

I'm grateful to the countless people who have taught me what I know about relationships. I learned those lessons at the cost of greatly inconveniencing many of those people. I know I can repay them only by sharing what I've learned with others.

For what I have learned about mutually loving relationships, I am inexpressibly indebted to my wife, Donna.

Table of Contents

Obstacles to Love and Solutions

Exercises and Stuff

Introduction

Mankind possesses an astonishing body of knowledge and power. We cure disease, travel in space, and casually speak to each other from opposite sides of the globe. We manipulate sub-atomic particles and create new forms of life.

But despite all that, most of us are not genuinely happy, and we prove that every day with our behavior. We say unkind things to and about our spouses, children, and co-workers. We shake our fists at each other on the highway and sue each other in court. Our children are angry, rebellious, using drugs, having sex, and otherwise declaring their misery. We can't build prisons quickly enough to accommodate the unhappy people who violate our laws. Half the marriages in this country end in divorce, and most of us who stay married are not experiencing the kind of happiness we once hoped to find. Most of us are afraid, angry, and alone — and we don't know what to do about it.

Fortunately, the cause of all this unhappiness is not complicated, nor is the solution. We simply don't know how to have loving relationships. Without loving relationships, we feel a painful emptiness that we then attempt to fill with money, possessions, power, approval, alcohol, drugs, and sex. Desperately, we hope that these things will bring us happiness, but they never do.

Delightfully, our situation is far from hopeless. We can all learn how to love each other and how to live without fear and anger. We will then discover powerfully loving relationships and a lasting happiness that we never imagined.

Although married couples are used for many of the examples of relationships in this book, these principles apply to relationships with friends, parents, children, and business associates.

I recommend three other books as useful companions to this one: *The Wart King,* The Truth About Love and Lies; *The Wise Man,* Telling the Truth and Finding Love; and *The Truth About Parenting*, A Simple and Powerfully Effective Way for Everyone to Raise Happy and Responsible Children.

The Truth About Relationships

Chapter 1

What Goes Wrong
In Relationships

Relationships fail all around us every day — between spouses, lovers, siblings, friends, co-workers, and so on. But despite the abundance of self-assured finger-pointing, the people involved rarely have any idea what actually went wrong, and they prove that as they blindly repeat the same mistakes over and over. Most people seem to be caught in an endless cycle of disappointment and unhappiness as they associate with other human beings.

When Christopher and Lisa met, they fell in love immediately. Six months later they got married and fully expected to be ecstatically happy for the rest of their lives. But in the first year of their marriage, there were already signs that the magic of their relationship was escaping them. They began to find fault with each other over little things. Roses and kisses were gradually replaced by expectations and disappointments, each of which left a wound and then a scar. Slowly, the excitement of being in love became a distant memory.

What happened here? How did the hopes and dreams of these delightful people get lost? Christopher and Lisa poured their whole hearts into making their relationship work. They didn't hold anything back — as most people don't — and still they failed. Understanding this is critical, because what happened with this couple is typical of what happens in virtually all unhappy relationships — between lovers, family members, people in the workplace, and so on. We've all had the experience of starting relationships that seemed promising and hopeful, only to have something go wrong that we didn't understand, leaving us feeling disappointed or worse. Until we do understand what happens in these situations, we're doomed to repeat the process again and again.

What Happened?
The Lie

As I discuss relationships throughout the book, I will refer to the participants in any interaction, however brief, as "partners."

As Lisa became increasingly unhappy in her marriage, she naturally blamed Christopher. We all tend to blame our partners — spouses, friends, children, even complete strangers — when we get upset, mostly because that's what we've seen everyone around us do. All our lives, we've heard countless variations on these statements: "You make me so mad," and "He (or she) makes me angry." We've heard those claims so many times that we've come to completely accept the notion that other people determine how we feel. If someone does something to inconvenience us or fails to do what we want, we immediately believe that they *make* us feel disappointed or angry.

But that belief is a lie, a lie we unintentionally use to relieve our own sense of helplessness and confusion when we feel bad and need someone to blame. Until we see that, we cannot learn to have loving and lasting relationships.

What Really Happened?
The Truth

It's quite understandable that Lisa made Christopher responsible for the unhappiness she felt in their marriage. He was certainly the closest available person to blame. But that still doesn't mean he *caused* her feelings. The truth is Lisa was unhappy *before* she got married. Christopher didn't do anything to *make* Lisa unhappy. He didn't beat her, or yell at her, or abuse her in any way. Christopher simply failed to provide what Lisa needed to make her happy, and when he failed, she blamed him for both the disappointment of their marriage *and* for the unhappiness she felt long before they met.

That's what happens in most relationships. When our partners fail to make us happy, we blame them for all the unhappiness in our lives, including the unhappiness we carried with us from the many years before we ever knew them. We make our partners scapegoats for everything we don't like. How terribly unfair that is, and what an awful effect that has on any relationship.

Imagine that after a violent storm and shipwreck, you and I are stranded on a barren island in the middle of the ocean. After a week with nothing to eat, I begin to complain that you aren't doing enough to provide food for me, and the hungrier I become, the more I whine. Not an hour goes by that I don't remind you that I'm starving, and that you are to blame.

You must think I'm insane. Did you cause my hunger? Of course not. I'm starving because there was a storm that wrecked our ship and left us stranded on an island without food — and you had nothing to do with any of that.

And so it is with relationships. When we're unhappy in a relationship, our misery is not the fault of our partner. We're unhappy because we're starving. We're missing the one ingredient most essential to genuine happiness, and it was missing long before we met our partner.

What We All Really Need

What we all need most — the one thing which creates happiness and fulfilling relationships — *is Real Love*, or unconditional love. It really is that simple. When we learn what Real Love is and when we find it, our unhappiness disappears just as surely as hunger vanishes in the presence of food. Loving relationships then become natural and effortless. I'll be talking a great deal more about how to find Real Love in the following chapters.

Blaming and Demands

My blaming you for my hunger after the shipwreck was not only inaccurate, but ineffective — it did nothing to help our predicament. It is a simple fact that two starving people with no source of food *can't* give each other what they need. No amount of expectation, disappointment, blaming, anger, or manipulation can change that.

And again, it's the same with relationships. When we're unhappy in a relationship, all the anger and blaming that we commonly exchange with our partners are completely wasteful and destructive. And it's foolish to insist that our partner *promised* to make us happy — as in a marriage vow. Our demands don't magically make them capable of doing anything.

Two people who are emotionally and spiritually starving in a relationship simply cannot make each other happy, no matter how hard they try. Each of them must find that one thing — Real Love — without which genuine happiness and loving relationships are quite impossible.

Abusive Relationships

Although I used the example of a non-abusive relationship with Christopher and Lisa, I recognize that many people *are* involved in verbally, physically, sexually, and emotionally abusive relationships. Even in those circumstances, the absence of unconditional love is still the primary problem, and Real Love is the prescription for everyone who wishes to find genuine happiness and loving relationships.

Chapter Summary

We tend to blame our partners for the unhappiness we experience in our relationships, when the real problem is the lack of unconditional love in our own lives.

Chapter 2

Real Love

Real Love is caring about the happiness of another person without any thought for what we might get for ourselves. Real Love is unaffected by the mistakes and flaws of the people we love. When they give us nothing in return — including gratitude — or even when they're thoughtless and inconsiderate, we're not disappointed, hurt, or angry, because our concern is for *their* happiness. Real Love is unconditional.

It's Real Love when someone cares about *our* happiness without any concern whatever for themselves. It's Real Love when people are not disappointed or angry when we make our foolish mistakes, even when we inconvenience them personally. Sadly, very few of us have ever seen love like that.

Real Love is An Absolute Requirement for Happiness

Prior to the late eighteenth century, sailors on long voyages often suffered from bleeding gums, tooth loss, and wounds that didn't heal. Many of them died. The physicians of the day called the condition scurvy, and they tried to treat it with better food, exercise, hygiene, and medical care. But nothing worked until they added citrus fruits to the sailors' diets. Scurvy then vanished completely, and eventually, we learned that it was all caused by a deficiency of a single molecule — vitamin C. Without it, people starved and died, even though their bellies were full of bread and beef.

Similarly, most of us are emotionally sick and dying from a deficiency we have not yet identified. We try to fill our sense of emptiness with money, power, food, approval, sex, and entertainment, but no matter how much of those things we acquire, we remain empty, alone, afraid, and angry. What we need is Real Love. Without it, we can only be miserable. With it, our happiness is absolutely guaranteed.

When I use the word "happiness," I do not mean the fleeting pleasure we get from money, sex, praise, and worldly success. Nor do I mean the brief feeling of relief we experience during the temporary absence of conflict or disaster. Real happiness is not the feeling we get from being entertained or making people do what we want. Genuine happiness is a profound and lasting sense of peace and fulfillment that deeply satisfies and enlarges the soul. It doesn't go away when circumstances get difficult. It survives and even grows through hardship and struggle. True happiness is our entire reason to live.

With Real Love, nothing else matters; without it, nothing else is enough.

The Connection and Life-Giving Power of Real Love

The greatest fear of all for a human being is to be unloved and alone. As a physician, I saw that confirmed many times by people who knew they were dying. Those people were consistently more afraid that no one cared about them and that they would die alone than they were of death itself.

But when someone is genuinely concerned about our happiness, we feel a strong connection to them. We feel included in their life, and in that instant, we are *no longer alone*. Each moment of unconditional acceptance creates a living thread to the person who accepts us. Those threads weave a powerful bond that fills us with a genuine and lasting happiness. Nothing but Real Love can do that. In addition, when one person loves us, we feel a connection to everyone else. We feel included in the family of all mankind, of which that one person is a part.

Imagine living in a world where all the people are truly happy. In this place there is no fear or anger. The people here are so filled with love and happiness that their only concern as they interact with you is *your* happiness, and you can feel that with absolute certainty. Because they have everything that really matters in life, they don't need you to do anything for them. So there is nothing you can do to disappoint them.

As you communicate with these people, you can see that it doesn't matter to them whether you're smart or pretty or handsome. You don't have to do anything to impress them or get them to like you. And they truly don't care if you make mistakes or say something stupid. It finally and powerfully occurs to you that it's impossible to be embarrassed or ashamed around these people — because they love you no matter what you do.

That is the feeling of being unconditionally loved — and many of us can't imagine it. We've been judged, criticized, and conditionally supported for so long that the idea of being unconditionally accepted is inconceivable. But I have seen what happens when people consistently take the steps that lead to finding Real Love (Chapters 7-11). They find a happiness that utterly transforms their lives. This is not a fantasy. Thousands of people have successfully used this simple process by which we can all learn to find Real Love, genuine happiness, and fulfilling relationships.

The Effect of Not Feeling Loved

Without Real Love, we feel empty, alone, and afraid. We can't tolerate those feelings, and we'll do *anything* to get rid of them. From the time we were small children, we all learned behaviors that made us feel good temporarily and gave us a sense of relief from our emptiness and fear: winning the approval of other people, getting angry, criticizing people, having sex, making money, controlling people, drinking alcohol, using drugs, and running from difficult relationships, to name just a few. *All the unproductive things we do with each other in relationships — lying, criticizing, anger, withdrawing, and so on — are just reactions to the pain of not feeling loved.* That doesn't excuse the foolish and hurtful things we do, but it does explain them. Not feeling unconditionally loved has terrible consequences.

Drowning

Imagine yourself again in the middle of the ocean (p. 7). But this time, there's no island, no one to help you, no lifeboat — and you're drowning. You're exhausted and terrified. Suddenly, a man grabs you from behind and pulls you under the water. Completely overwhelmed by fear and anger, you struggle wildly to get free, but your efforts are unsuccessful, and you remain underwater.

Just as you're about to pass out and drown, I arrive in a boat and pull you from the water. After catching your breath, you turn to see that the man who pulled you under the water is also drowning, and it's obvious now that he only grabbed you in an attempt to keep his own head above water. He wasn't trying to harm you at all. Knowing that, your anger vanishes immediately, and you quickly help him into the boat.

Let's examine what we can learn from this imagined experience — about ourselves and about other people.

Why do other people hurt us?

Only moments before I arrived, you were absolutely certain that the man in the water was a killer. Sitting in the safety of the boat, however, you determined with a single glance that he wasn't trying to hurt *you* at all. He was only trying to save *himself*.

And so it is in relationships. People really don't do things with the goal of hurting *us*. When people hurt us, they're simply drowning and trying to save *themselves*. People who don't feel unconditionally loved are desperate and will do anything to eliminate the pain of their emptiness. Unfortunately, as they struggle to get the things that give them temporary relief—approval, money, sex, power, etc. —their behavior often has a negative effect on the people around them, including us. But that is not their first intent.

Other people hurt us only because they are reacting badly to the pain of feeling unloved and alone. When we truly understand that, our feelings toward people, and our relationships with them, change dramatically.

Why do we hurt other people?

When the drowning man first grabbed you from behind, you were understandably angry at him, believing that he was trying to kill you. In fact, you fought to free yourself, and if you had been strong enough, you could have drowned him.

And again, it's the same in relationships. Without Real Love, we feel like we're drowning all the time. In that condition, almost everything seems threatening to us, even the most innocent behaviors. When people get angry or criticize us, we don't see them as drowning and protecting themselves. We become afraid and defend ourselves, using behaviors that often result in injury to others.

It is not our primary goal to hurt the people around us. But when we don't feel unconditionally loved —when we're drowning —we're desperate. We don't think clearly as we do things to feel better and protect ourselves. And those things often hurt other people.

Why do we get angry?

One of the ways we hurt people is to get angry at them and blame them for our anger. But *other people never "make" us angry.* If we all understood and remembered that one principle, very few relationships would fail. Most relationships fall apart because we angrily blame our partners for something they did or did not do. We need to remember that our anger is really a reaction to a lifetime of trying to survive without unconditional love. That's enough to make anyone angry. We get angry because then we feel less helpless and afraid. Anger protects us and briefly makes us feel better.

Lisa (p. 5) wasn't angry because of anything Christopher did in the few months they were together. She was unhappy and discouraged because of a lifetime not feeling loved. You weren't murderously angry at the man in the water because of a single tug on your shoulder. You were angry because you'd been spit out in the middle of the ocean with no chance for survival, and because you were exhausted and frightened and about to die. Anger makes much more sense when we see the real cause for it.

In relationships, we only get angry because we don't feel loved. In that painful condition, we lash out at anything that threatens us — which is almost everything. Anger is terribly destructive to relationships, but when we're drowning, we don't react reasonably to the situation at hand; we react to many years of emptiness and pain, and we protect ourselves from every imaginable threat to our safety.

As we find Real Love, it's like being pulled out of the water into a boat. Our fear and anger simply vanish. Loving relationships then become natural and easy.

And all the other stupid things we do

We do so many stupid things in response to the pain of not feeling loved. We use money, power, sex, praise, approval, drugs, and alcohol. We cheat on our spouses. We criticize people and blame them for our feelings. We argue with those we love and insist on being right. We withdraw from those who might hurt us, even though that separates us from the very people we want to be close to. We even pick up guns and shoot each other. We do all those things to minimize the pain of feeling unloved, and we'll discuss them more in the next two chapters.

When you understood that the man in the water was not trying to hurt you and was only trying to save himself, your anger disappeared, and you were glad to help him into the boat. You had no more desire to struggle against him or hurt him. When we feel unconditionally loved, we also lose the need to protect ourselves and do the things which hurt our partners. That makes a huge difference in relationships.

My own experience with drowning

I know something about drowning. Having insufficient unconditional love in my life, I spent a lifetime acquiring money, power, and the approval of others. No matter how much I earned, those things completely failed to make me happy. Despite having what the world called a successful life, I was desperate for relief from the pain of feeling empty and alone, and I turned to some very foolish solutions for my discomfort. I became a drug addict for years and caused great harm to my wife and children. I became depressed and suicidal. People who are drowning don't think clearly. They hurt themselves and everyone around them.

We Have Not Been Loved Unconditionally

Most of us have received little, if any, Real Love. We prove that every day with our unhappiness — our fear, anger, blaming, withdrawal, manipulation, controlling, etc. People who feel unconditionally loved don't feel and do those things.

As a child, I was thrilled when my mother smiled at me, spoke softly, and held me. I knew from those **behaviors** that she loved me. I also noticed that she did those pleasant things more often when I was "good" — when I was quiet, grateful, and cooperative. In other words, I saw that she loved me more when I did what she enjoyed, something almost all parents understandably do.

When I was "bad" — noisy, disobedient, and otherwise inconvenient — she did not speak softly or smile at me. On those occasions, she frowned, sighed with disappointment, and often spoke with a harsh tone. *Although it was unintentional,* she clearly told me with those behaviors that she loved me less, and that was the worst pain in the world for me.

Nearly all of us were loved that way. When we made the football team, got good grades, and washed the dishes without being asked, our parents naturally looked happy and said things like, "Way to go!" or "I'm so proud of you." But when we failed a class at school, or tracked dog poop across the carpet, or wrecked the car, or fought with our siblings, did our parents smile at us then? Did they pat us on the shoulder and speak kindly as they corrected us? No, with rare exceptions, they did not. Without thinking, they frowned, rolled their eyes, and sighed with exasperation. They used a tone of voice that was *not* the one we heard when we did what they wanted and made them look good. Some of us were even yelled at or physically abused when we were "bad."

Other people in our childhood gave us the same conditional approval. School teachers smiled and encouraged us when we were bright and cooperative, but they behaved quite differently when we were slow and difficult. Even our own friends liked us more when we did what they liked. In fact, that's what made them our friends. And that pattern of conditional approval has continued throughout our lives.

Picture in your mind some of the people close to you — parents, children, spouse, friends — and predict the expression on their faces ...

if you completely forgot their birthday.

if they said "hello" to you and you responded by walking away and angrily mumbling something under your breath.

if you were an hour late for a special dinner they had prepared for you.

if you got them nothing for Christmas after they had spent a great deal of time and money buying a gift for you.

if you snapped at them after they'd said something quite innocent to you.

Do you honestly imagine that they'd smile and be delighted with you if you did those things? Of course not. In almost every case, they'd be disappointed and unhappy. In addition, most of them would probably be hurt and angry—which would be entirely understandable. However, such reactions clearly demonstrate the conditional nature of their love.

Real Love is, "I care how **you** feel." Conditional love is, "I like how you make **me** feel." Conditional love is what people have given to us when we did what they wanted, and it's the only kind of love that most of us have ever known. People have liked us more when we made them feel good, or at least when we did nothing to inconvenience them. It was natural and unintentional that our parents and others did that, and they did it from the time we were small babies.

Although it is given unintentionally, conditional acceptance has an unspeakably disastrous effect because it fails to form the bonds of human connection created by Real Love. No matter how much conditional love we receive, we still feel empty, alone, and miserable. Tragically, most of us have filled our lives with that empty "love," and *that* is the real reason we're now unhappy in our relationships—not because of anything our present partners have done or have not done. This principle is easily important enough to repeat: if you're unhappy, don't look at your partner for the cause. You're unhappy because you don't feel unconditionally loved, and that's been going on for a long time, usually from early childhood.

Blaming Our Parents
vs.
Understanding Our Past

In our emotional development as children, there was nothing more important than a supply of Real Love. Without it, we were guaranteed to become empty, frightened, and unhappy adults. While it's useful to *understand* that our parents were responsible for loving us as children, and are therefore responsible for a great deal of how we function now, it's very unproductive to *blame* them if we're unhappy now. *Understanding* is a simple assessment of how things are, while *blaming* is an angry attitude that can only be harmful to us and to others.

Although our parents had an enormous impact on our lives, *we* are solely responsible for the choices we make now. Continued resentment and anger will not help us make wise decisions in the present. In addition, blaming our parents is especially inappropriate when we understand that *they gave us the best they had.* I've never met a parent who got up in the morning and thought, "Today I could unconditionally love and teach my children and fill their lives with joy. But no, I think I'll be selfish, critical, and demanding instead." Our parents loved us as well as they could. If they failed to give us the Real Love we needed, it was only because they didn't have it to give. If *they* weren't unconditionally loved, they couldn't possibly have given us the Real Love we required.

Cheryl was very unhappy, and she blamed it all on her husband. When a wise friend explained to her the real cause of her condition — that she was not unconditionally loved as a child — she said, "But my parents did love me!"

Friend: "How often did your father hold you and tell you he loved you? How many times each day was he obviously delighted when you entered the room? How often did your mother sit with you and ask what was happening in your life — just to listen, not to give advice?"

Cheryl was speechless. Although she was raised by parents as good as any she knew, she couldn't think of a single time when any of those things had happened.

Friend: "What happened when you made mistakes and disappointed your parents? Did you feel just as loved then as when you were 'good?'"

As Cheryl described the details of her childhood, it was obvious that her father mostly avoided her. Her mother was kind when Cheryl was obedient, but she was critical and harsh when Cheryl "misbehaved." Cheryl realized that she had never been corrected and loved at the same time. Her wise friend made it clear that there was no blaming in this, just an attempt to understand the real cause of the fear and anger in her life. She could then begin to take the steps necessary to find Real Love (Chapter 7) instead of blaming her husband, which was ruining her marriage and making her very unhappy.

How Do We Get Real Love?

If Real Love is so very important, how do we find it?

The Wart King

Once there was a rich and beautiful kingdom that stretched beyond the horizon in all directions. But the prince of that kingdom was very unhappy. He had warts all over his face, and everywhere he went, people teased him and laughed at him. So he mostly stayed in his room, alone and miserable.

Upon the death of his father, the prince became king and issued a decree that no one — on pain of death — would ever laugh at his warts again. But still he stayed in his room, ashamed and alone. On the rare occasions that he did go out, he put a cloth bag over his head, which covered his warts but also made it difficult for him to see.

After many years, the king heard about a wise man living on the top of a nearby mountain. Hoping the wise man could help him, the king climbed the mountain and found the old man sitting under a tree. Taking the bag off his head, the king said, "I've come for your help."

The wise man looked intently at the king for several long moments and finally said, "You have warts on your face."

The king was enraged. That was not what he'd come to hear. "No, I don't," he screamed. Ashamed and angry, he put the bag back over his head.

"Yes, you do," said the wise man, gently.

"I'll have you killed!" shouted the king.

"Call your guards then," said the wise man.

"My guards aren't here!" shrieked the king helplessly. "I climbed all the way up this mountain to get your help, and now you tell me I have warts on my face?! How cruel you are!"

Angry and frustrated, the king ran from the wise man, falling repeatedly because he couldn't see very well with the bag on his head. Finally, the king fell down a steep slope and into a lake, where he began to drown. The wise man jumped in, pulled the king to shore, and took the bag from his head so he could breathe.

The king was horrified when he saw the wise man staring at him. "You're laughing at me," said the king.

"Not at all," said the wise man, smiling.

With his eyes fixed on the ground, the king said, "The boys in the village laughed at me."

The old man immediately responded: "I'm not one of the boys in the village. That must have been hard for you, being laughed at."

"Yes, it was," admitted the king, with tears in his eyes.

"As you can see, I'm not laughing at you," repeated the wise man.

Somehow this did feel different to the king. As he looked into the lake, he saw his reflection. "I really do have a lot of warts."

"I know," said the wise man.

"And you don't find them disgusting?"

"No, and I don't find my own warts disgusting anymore, either."

The king noticed for the first time that the wise man also had warts. "Why do *you* not wear a bag over your head?"

"I used to," replied the old man. "But with the bag on my head, I couldn't see. And I was lonely. So I took it off."

"Didn't people laugh at you?" asked the king.

"Oh sure, some did. And I hated that, like you do. But gradually I found a few people who didn't laugh, and that made me very happy."

The king was thrilled. No one had ever looked at his warts without laughing at him or showing their disgust. "I think I won't wear the bag when you're around."

The wise man smiled. "When you go home, you might even leave the bag here."

The king wondered aloud, "Will I find other people like you, who won't think I'm disgusting?"

The wise man laughed. "Of course you will. And with the love of those people, you won't care when other people laugh."

The king dropped the bag on the ground and went back to his kingdom, which was far more beautiful without the bag on his head. And he did find people who didn't mind his warts at all. He was very happy.

Like the Wart King, we've all learned that people express their affection far less when they see our many mistakes and flaws, especially the ones that inconvenience them. So we hide our flaws, which enables us to avoid criticism but also makes it impossible for people to see who we really are. Hiding under the bags we've put on our heads, we briefly feel safer, but we also feel quite alone, which is the worst condition of all.

The Process of Feeling Loved
Truth → Seen → Accepted → Loved

When we hide who we are — figuratively wearing bags on our heads — we can only feel alone and miserable. When we tell the **truth** about ourselves, we can be **seen** by others as we really are. And then we can feel genuinely **accepted** by people and believe that they truly care about *our* happiness, which is the definition of **Real Love**. In short, we create the opportunity to feel loved when we tell the truth about ourselves, as the Wart King did.

Only when we take the bags off our heads — when we tell the truth about ourselves, especially about our mistakes and flaws — can we find people to accept and love us in the same way the Wise Man did for the Wart King. The effect is miraculous, even when we feel accepted and loved for only short periods of time. A wise man (or woman) is anyone who feels sufficiently loved himself that he is capable of accepting and loving us when he sees the truth about us. We'll discuss the role of wise men — and how we can all become wise men and women — throughout the book.

Real Love vs. Conditional Love

The ability to distinguish Real Love and conditional love is critical. When we can't do that, we tend to settle for giving and receiving conditional love, leaving us empty and confused. Fortunately, there are two reliable signs that love is not genuine: **disappointment** and **anger**. Every time we frown, sigh with disappointment, speak harshly, or in any way express our anger at someone, we're communicating that we didn't get what **we** wanted — and that's not caring for **their** happiness (Real Love).

Our disappointment and anger absolutely prove that our concern in that moment is for ourselves, not for the happiness of our partner — and that's conditional love. Our partners then sense our selfishness and feel disconnected from us and alone, regardless of whatever else we say or give to them.

We self-righteously like to believe that we're genuinely loving when we're not. That illusion evaporates when we consider how many times a day we feel disappointed or critical when people don't behave in a way that pleases us — the cardinal sign of conditional love. We become annoyed with our spouses when they don't give us what we want. We get irritated at other drivers who slow our progress on the road. We're impatient when we have to wait in a long line. We're disappointed in our children when they behave badly. We're annoyed when people are late, ungrateful, and otherwise inconvenient. The list is endless, and it all proves that we don't feel unconditionally loving toward others, at least not in the moment of our impatience. It's also further evidence that we don't feel unconditionally loved ourselves.

Of course, this means of judging conditional love works both ways. If other people are disappointed or angry with us, they can't be loving us unconditionally, either.

But . . .

At this point, many people think or say, "*But* according to your definition, I don't know anyone who is really loving. Everyone I know gets disappointed or angry when people are ungrateful, thoughtless, and rude. Are you saying the whole world's understanding of love is wrong?" Yes, I am. While we claim to be loving, we yell at each other on the highway, take each other to court, get divorced, go to war, drink alcohol, take drugs, neglect our children, and quarrel with each other over the smallest things. Most of us walk around in a constant state of irritation, or at least we can be provoked to anger very easily. These behaviors are undeniable proof that we don't feel loved, nor can we give Real Love.

Disappointment and anger are always selfish. Hearing that, many people justify themselves with another *but*. They protest, "But we can't just unconditionally love people when they're wrong. Somebody has to speak up when mistakes are made." Sometimes we do have the responsibility to teach and correct people — children and employees, for example. But that never has to be done with disappointment and anger, the two signs that always reveal that our true motivation is to get something for ourselves — and that is not Real Love.

Loving unconditionally does not mean giving people everything they want. That's just indulgence and spoiling. Many examples of giving unconditional acceptance and correction at the same time are found in the rest of the book.

One More Thing:
Real Love and an Understanding of Right and Wrong

Understanding Real Love enables us to settle a very important issue, one that philosophers and theologians have argued for centuries: the question of right and wrong. Being genuinely happy (p. 10) is the ultimate goal in life and also the ultimate good. Because Real Love is absolutely essential to our happiness, I suggest that anything which interferes with our ability to feel unconditionally loved and to share that love with others is therefore bad or wrong. We'll discuss those bad things in Chapters 3 and 4.

Chapter Summary

Real Love is caring about the happiness of another person — with no thought for our own reward. Real Love is "I care how **you** feel." Conditional love is "I like how you make **me** feel."

Real Love creates a powerful bond between people that always leads to genuine happiness. Without Real Love, people can only feel empty, alone, afraid, and angry.

Most of us were loved conditionally, which explains the unhappiness we experience now as adults.

We can all find Real Love as we learn to tell the truth about ourselves to people who are capable of unconditionally accepting and loving us. Such people are called wise men and wise women.

Real Love can be distinguished from conditional love by the absence of disappointment and anger.

Chapter 3

Imitation Love

Without Real Love, our emptiness is intolerably painful. We're starving to death, and we'll do anything to eliminate our discomfort — even if the relief we obtain is quite temporary and the overall effect of our behavior is destructive to ourselves and others. We attempt to fill our emptiness with whatever feels good in the moment. We use money, the approval of others, anger, sex, alcohol, drugs, violence, etc., all of which are variations of only four general things: praise, power, pleasure, and safety. When these things are used as substitutes for Real Love — as they almost always are — I call them Imitation Love.

Praise

There are many kinds of praise: flattery, gratitude, respect, sex, and money, among others.

Flattery

When people tell us how wonderful we are, we temporarily believe we're worthwhile. In the absence of Real Love, we convince ourselves that flattery is genuine affection instead of seeing it for what it really is: praise that we have to earn. We spend countless hours and dollars on make-up, hair-styling, clothing, plastic surgery, and exercise, all in the hope that someone will say, "You look great." We work hard at school, in our jobs, and at home in the hope that people will compliment our intelligence, creativity, and diligence. Our obsession with winning — in sports, business, and even everyday arguments — is also motivated by a desire to be flattered.

Gratitude

We love it when people say "Thank you" to us. We take it as a form of praise. It makes us feel important. In fact, we often do things for people just so we can receive their gratitude. We prove that every time we're disappointed and even angry on the occasions when we *don't* receive an expression of appreciation for something we've done for someone else.

People who feel unconditionally loved don't require gratitude for the things they do. Their concern is for the happiness of other people. With Real Love, they already have what matters most, so they don't need any reward, including gratitude, for what they do.

Respect

Many of us work long hours, make great sacrifices, worry, scheme, and manipulate people, all for the purpose of creating an image that will be admired at work and elsewhere. We want people to respect us as capable and strong. People who feel unconditionally loved don't need that, but in the absence of Real Love, the respect of others is very important.

Sex

We've been taught by the media and our peers that people pay us the ultimate compliment when they find us sexually attractive. And we believe it. Many of us will do almost anything to be praised for our for sexual desirability.

Money and Success

We tend to judge people by their financial success, and we prove that with our endless curiosity about each other's jobs, incomes, investments, houses, cars, boats, etc. We love to be praised for our accomplishments. Most of us can't even have a conversation with a relative stranger without asking, "What do you do for a living?" When the response is, "I'm the chief executive officer of a Fortune 500 corporation," we're mightily impressed. But our reaction is considerably less enthusiastic when we're told that our companion is a housewife or street sweeper. What an indictment that is of our need to be praised.

We hope that money and success will make us deserving of approval, which we then wishfully interpret as a kind of affection. It's only Imitation Love, but in the absence of Real Love, it feels pretty good, and many of us are quite willing to devote our entire lives to the pursuit of it.

The Emptiness of Praise and All Imitation Love

When people say nice things to us, we feel good. But we've all learned from considerable experience that people praise us only when we're doing what they like. We then have to work hard to keep pleasing them and earning their approval. We're trapped. Earning praise becomes a never-ending burden, costing us far more than we get from it. And that's true with every form of Imitation Love.

The pursuit of Imitation Love may seem exciting and fruitful in the beginning, but the excitement always wears off. Earning Imitation Love invariably becomes exhausting and frustrating, and it never makes us truly happy.

Power

In the absence of Real Love, we usually define power as the ability to influence the behavior of people and things. We use money, authority, sex, flattery, and personal persuasion to influence, control, and even hurt people. We actually feel some sense of connection to the people we control. The bond is shallow and fleeting, but it feels better than the pain of being completely alone. We also feel an emotional excitement during those moments of power.

Authority

When we have a position of authority — in business, politics, the family, and other organizations — we can often make people do what we want, and then we feel less of the terrible helplessness that always accompanies the lack of unconditional love in our lives. As people follow our direction, we also persuade ourselves that somehow they approve of us, something we want badly. In addition, we enjoy feeling strong as we tell people what to do.

Money

We can really make things happen with money, and we like that. Money makes trucks move, planes take off, and people scurry to satisfy our desires. We can even buy friends. But the power of money is a mirage which vanishes easily. Ask anyone who has suffered a great financial loss. Or ask someone who still has more money than he or she can ever use and has discovered the emptiness of it. Money can never buy unconditional love, the only thing that will ever make us genuinely happy.

Sex

Imagine a young girl who gets little or no respect from her parents, teachers, and even her peers. She feels alone and helpless. But if she becomes sexually attractive, she quickly discovers that she can use her appearance and sexual behavior to influence and even control the thoughts and behavior of boys and men in a very powerful way. It's an exciting and seductive experience.

Pleasure

When Real Love is missing, sex, food, travel, wealth, and other forms of entertainment provide a welcome distraction from our emptiness and pain.

Excitement

Playing or watching a game of basketball *can* be exciting in a healthy way. Seeing the earth from a plane at 32,000 feet can be stirring to the soul. But most of us seek excitement as a *substitute* for real happiness, not as an addition to the love and lasting fulfillment we already enjoy in our lives. When we play video games night and day, watch violent movies, take mind-altering drugs, and look for ways to "live on the edge," our goal is often to achieve distraction from our otherwise unfulfilling lives. We don't want to face our personal emptiness and our inability to find and maintain loving relationships. We use excitement to replace the Real Love we need and don't have.

Sex

Sexual gratification is an unbelievably widespread addiction. Many of us are obsessed with being sexually attractive and achieving the next sexual experience. People fantasize about sex constantly. Every day, millions of us search for sexual stimulation on the Internet. We read books and go to movies for sexual excitement. Sex is a powerful form of pleasure, but without Real Love, it's just as empty and deceptive as all the other forms of Imitation Love.

Safety

Without Real Love, we're already in the worst kind of pain, and we're willing to do anything to keep it from increasing. One way to minimize the risk of being hurt is to avoid doing anything unfamiliar. So we stay in the same boring jobs, attempt to learn nothing new, and continue in stagnant, unrewarding — but predictable — relationships. When we're not being actively injured by something or someone, we confuse that safety with real happiness.

The Danger of Imitation Love

In the absence of Real Love, we often allow ourselves to believe that we're actually loved and happy when we get enough Imitation Love. But no matter how much of it we acquire, we never get the feeling of connection with other people that happens with Real Love, so we're still alone. An ocean of Imitation Love lacks the power to create the happiness found in a teaspoon of the real thing.

The world is filled with miserable people who have accumulated mountains of Imitation Love: flattery, gratitude, position, respect, sex, and money. Those people have proven beyond all doubt that Imitation Love cannot produce real happiness. Nonetheless, we frantically continue to trade Imitation Love with each other because it does feel good for a moment — much like a snort of cocaine makes an addict feel "good" for a short time. *That* is the danger of Imitation Love, that it feels good enough that we spend our lives for it. We trade our lives for nothing.

The Attraction of Imitation Love

If Imitation Love leaves us feeling empty and miserable, why do we keep pursuing it? Because living without unconditional love and feeling alone are unbearable, and we'll do *anything* to get rid of those feelings, however superficial and temporary the relief might be.

Chuck was fifteen years old. His mother told him every day — often without words — that he was messy and a huge inconvenience to her. His father told him he was clumsy and irresponsible. Understandably, Chuck felt unimportant, unloved, empty, and alone. And then he discovered that Melanie, a fourteen-year-old girl down the street, thought he was cute. Wow! She actually thought he was smart and liked to be with him. He suddenly felt important and powerful. He also enjoyed the excitement of physically touching her and eventually having sex with her. All this Imitation Love was more attention than he'd ever gotten, and he loved it, clinging to it like a drowning man.

When Chuck's parents learned he was having sex with Melanie, they angrily forbade him to see her again. It's no surprise that he stubbornly ignored their commands. He was not about to let go of the only thing he had ever found that had ever relieved the intolerable emptiness and pain in his life. That reasoning didn't justify his behavior, but it certainly explained it.

Imitation Love and Conditional Love

Conditional love is the approval that people give to us when we do what they want. Throughout the book, I will use *Imitation Love* as a term which describes everything that takes the place of Real Love and makes us feel good in its absence — praise, power, pleasure, safety *and* the conditional love of others. Because the term *Imitation Love* **includes** *conditional love*, I will use the first term rather than the second to describe those interactions where love is conditional.

Praise, Power, Pleasure, Safety
and Real Love

I'm not saying that praise, power, pleasure, and safety are always bad. They're dangerous only when they're used as a substitute for Real Love and genuine happiness. When two people really care about each other's happiness, praise is nourishing and fun, not contrived and manipulative. Each partner experiences the real power of being loving and happy. Both partners feel safe. And sex becomes a natural expression of their love and a healthy pleasure.

Chapter Summary

We can't live with the pain of not feeling unconditionally loved. To lessen our discomfort, we use Imitation Love in the form of praise, power, pleasure, and safety.

Imitation Love never makes us genuinely happy, but it does feel good for a moment, and we're willing to spend our lives in the pursuit of it.

Chapter 4

Getting and Protecting Behaviors

The absence of unconditional love creates an emptiness that we cannot ignore. Our subsequent behavior is completely determined by our *need* to be loved and our *fear* of not being loved. We do whatever it takes — Getting Behaviors — to fill our sense of emptiness, and we use Protecting Behaviors to eliminate our fear.

Protecting Behaviors

We protect ourselves in four general ways: lying, attacking, acting like victims, and running. I'll briefly describe each of them here and will illustrate them in greater detail, with real-life examples, throughout the remainder of the book.

Lying

We've learned from countless experiences that when we inconvenience people with our mistakes, they tend to express their disappointment and anger toward us. We then feel less loved and more alone, the two feelings that terrify us the most. To keep that from happening, we lie about our mistakes. We hide who we really are, as the Wart King did (pp. 19-22).

Closely observe a conversation between any two people. Almost invariably, each of them carefully — and unconsciously — watches the other, looking for the first hint of disapproval: a brow wrinkling into a frown, an eyelid lifting into an expression of doubt, or a corner of the mouth turning down. And when that happens, the speaker immediately modifies what he's saying until all signs of disapproval are gone. That modification of what we say and do to please other people is lying — because we don't tell our partner that we're trying to get them to like us. In our defense, we don't even know that we're doing it in most cases.

We're also lying when we fail to take complete responsibility for what we do and how we feel. We do this so often, we think it's normal. Perhaps the most common example of this kind of lying is when we blame people for "making" us angry, a lie we exposed on pp. 6-7 and 14.

Attacking

Attacking is any behavior which motivates another person with *fear* to behave in a way we want. Attacking is a very effective form of protection. Criticism, anger, physical intimidation, and withdrawal of approval are common forms of attack. We've all seen many examples of each. Even people who appear to be the aggressors in a situation, who are "in control" and hurting other people, are often just protecting themselves with their attacks.

Acting like victims

Victims blame everyone but themselves for their own mistakes and unhappiness. They have excuses for everything, and we've all used this approach at some time. When we're confronted about a mistake we've made and say, "I couldn't help it," we're acting like victims. One battle cry of the victim is, "Look what you've done to me," an appeal to the sympathy of anyone who is hurting him, or who might do so. Victims always appear wounded and helpless, and it's an effective way to protect themselves from further injury.

Running

If we simply move away from a source of pain, we're less likely to be hurt. Withdrawing, avoiding people, leaving relationships, and being shy are all forms of running. Drugs and alcohol are other ways to run.

The Reward for Protecting

Safety is the payoff for all the Protecting Behaviors. We lie, attack people, act like victims, and run away so that other people won't criticize, attack, abandon, and otherwise hurt us. The Wart King used all those behaviors with the Wise Man.

Getting Behaviors

Imitation Love distracts us from the pain of feeling unloved. It temporarily makes us feel good. We get it by lying, attacking, acting like victims, and clinging.

Lying

Any time we make ourselves look good so people will like us, we're manipulating them — we're using them. Again, because we do this without telling them, we're lying — and we're usually not consciously aware of our lies. We lie so often that we've come to accept it as entirely normal. We just don't see it anymore. When we hide our mistakes or blame them on others, we're lying. When we tell people about our accomplishments but not our flaws, we're lying. When we hide how we really feel, we're lying. When we try to say what people want to hear, we're lying. And even when we modify our physical appearance so that people will be attracted to us, we're lying. With our lies, we buy praise, power, pleasure, and safety.

Attacking

When we manipulate people in any way that makes them afraid, that's attacking. For example, with anger — probably the most common form of attacking — we can make most people sufficiently uncomfortable (afraid) that they'll do whatever we want in order to stop us from making them feel bad. With our anger, we can get people to give us attention, respect, power, flattery, approval, and sex. As much as we hate to admit it, we effectively force these things from the people around us and we take them as a kind of affection. It's all Imitation Love, but it feels better than being completely alone. We use many other forms of attacking to get what we want: guilt, authority at work and home, criticism, and so on.

Act Like Victims

If we can convince people that we've been injured and treated unfairly, they'll often give us their sympathy, attention, and support. Victims are always loudly complaining about what people should have done for them, and they make people feel guilty if they don't do those things. It's an effective manipulation. What they get from that is only Imitation Love — because it's bought rather than freely given — but it feels better than nothing.

Clinging

When we hang on tightly to anyone who gives us attention, we can sometimes squeeze even more out of them. We often do this when we flatter the people who do things for us, or when we tell people how much we love them and need them. It's a manipulation we use — often unconsciously — to get more of what we want from them. Effectively, we're begging for more Imitation Love.

The Price of Getting and Protecting

With Getting and Protecting Behaviors, we do enjoy the temporary pleasure of Imitation Love, but the cost is very high.

Exhausting

Lying, being angry, and manipulating people for attention are a lot of work. And yet most of us give our entire lives to these hopelessly unfulfilling activities.

Addictive

Like the effect of an addictive drug, Imitation Love only feels good for a moment. Consider how briefly a word of praise makes us "happy," even though we may have worked hard for a very long time to earn it. The satisfaction is gone in an instant, and then we're back to wearing ourselves out again to earn the next kind word. In addition, increasing quantities of Imitation Love are required to achieve the same level of pleasure — just like an addictive drug. For example, getting a dollar was a big deal when we were five years old. But as we got older, it took more and more money to get that same thrill. And many of us are still pursuing that excitement, only to find that millions and even billions of dollars are not enough. The same addictive pattern is true with praise, sex, power, and so on.

Unloved

When we manipulate people in any way for something we want, what we get is purchased, not freely offered. We're paying for what we get. *It is impossible for us to feel unconditionally loved when we use Getting and Protecting Behaviors* (pp. 45-7).

Alone

We can never feel genuinely connected to someone while we're lying to them, blaming them, being angry at them, and protecting ourselves from them. All those activities drive us away from the people we want to be close to. We prove that conclusively every day. There are many brief rewards for using Getting and Protecting Behaviors, but they all leave us feeling more alone, which is the worst feeling of all.

Getting and Protecting are Mostly Unconscious

As terrible as Getting and Protecting Behaviors are, they are rarely intentional. A drowning man doesn't mean to hurt other people; in his state of mindless panic, he simply can't stop himself from grabbing anything or anyone that might help him keep his head above the water. His fear is so overwhelming that he doesn't think for a second about the harm he might cause others as he saves himself.

Without Real Love, our fear of being unloved and alone is overwhelming. We then use our Getting and Protecting Behaviors in a state of panic very similar to that of a drowning man. Our primary intent is not to hurt other people; our real goal is only to eliminate our own emptiness, fear, and pain. When we really understand that, the way we see our own behavior and the behavior of others changes forever.

The Elimination of Guilt and Anger

All our lives we've been taught that when we inconvenience and hurt other people, we're "bad," morally defective, even monstrous. We're supposed to feel guilty when we offend anyone. And we all feel entirely justified in being angry at those evil people who dare to violate all that is right and good by inconveniencing and hurting *us*. Our society virtually revolves around the principles of guilt and anger. *The guilty must pay*. If we are the guilty ones, we must feel great remorse and wallow in our guilt. If others have transgressed, then we feel justified in venting our anger against them.

But all that guilt and anger turn to dust when we understand our need for Real Love and our inevitable use of Getting and Protecting Behaviors when we don't have it. When we lie, attack people, act like victims, and run, it's not because we're bad or wish to hurt other people. We do those things because we're empty and afraid. We're doing the only things we know to protect ourselves and fill our lives with Imitation Love. That does not justify our behavior, but it certainly explains it.

It's a huge waste of time, energy, and happiness to wallow in guilt when we make mistakes. How much more productive it is to simply *see* our mistakes clearly and learn from them. In most cases, the problem is a lack of Real Love, which we can solve by taking some very simple steps (Chapters 7-11).

Similarly, when other people do things to inconvenience and hurt us, being angry at them is enormously foolish when we remember that they, too, are simply empty and afraid. They're only doing their best to deal with *their* pain, even though their best efforts are selfish and counter-productive. What those people need is someone to understand and help them. They don't need yet another person to be angry at them and punish them, which only adds to their pain and actually increases the likelihood that they'll use even more Getting and Protecting Behaviors. Anger and punishment do not make people happier. That does not mean there is no place for consequences, even prisons, something we'll discuss on pp. 150-1.

An Example of Getting and Protecting Behaviors

Despite a great job, plenty of money, a beautiful wife, and all the things that most people work for, Matthew was not happy. He tried therapy, self-help books, even going to church, but nothing worked — he was still discouraged and depressed.

Matthew's childhood didn't appear unusual. His parents stayed married to each other, and they didn't yell at him or beat him. But they did what almost all parents do: when Matthew was a "good" boy, they smiled and spoke kindly to him; when he was noisy, messy, and inconvenient, they frowned, spoke harshly, and emotionally withdrew from him.

Matthew had an essential need for unconditional love that was never filled. So he spent the rest of his life using Getting and Protecting Behaviors. As a small boy he learned to lie when he made mistakes. When he did that, he avoided the disapproval of his parents and others. When lying didn't work, he acted like a victim to get sympathy.

He studied diligently in school to get good grades and win the approval of his parents and teachers. He learned to use anger to get what he wanted from his siblings and his peers. He was a master of Getting and Protecting Behaviors by the time he left grade school.

Matthew didn't consciously realize that he was trying to earn everyone's affection, but it was still the central effort of his life and a burden that he carried everywhere he went. He was unwittingly living a lie for the purpose of earning praise, power, and pleasure for himself. When he did it well, he temporarily felt good, but he never got the Real Love he needed, so he still felt empty and alone.

As an adult, he continued the same behaviors he had learned as a child. He worked hard to get a good job and to earn the advancement in his career that would buy him the admiration and respect of his family and peers. When he made mistakes, he covered them up or blamed them on others, the same skills he had used as an infant. Or he used his position of authority — at work and at home — to intimidate people (attack) so they wouldn't confront him about his mistakes at all. If he felt sufficiently threatened by someone, he simply withdrew from the interaction or from the entire relationship (running).

Matthew was just reacting to his desperate need for Real Love and his fear that no one would ever love him. But with all his Getting and Protecting Behaviors, he didn't get any of the Real Love he desperately needed. In fact, his behavior made loving relationships impossible. Most of us are much like Matthew. When we understand that, we can begin to do something about it. We can find Real Love and begin to abandon the Getting and Protecting Behaviors that have such a devastating effect on our relationships and our happiness.

How Did the World Get Like This?

We all really do want to be loving toward each other — rather than demanding and hurtful — but we don't know how. Because we didn't get Real Love as children or as adults, we're empty and afraid, and in that condition, we can only see what others can do **for** us or **to** us. We see people as objects which either serve us or hurt us. Blinded by need and fear, we search for Imitation Love and protect ourselves with every interaction. We simply don't know how to love other people.

But haven't we all experienced moments when we did feel accepted and loved? Sure, many of us have, but those occasions were not enough to establish a consistent pattern and form positive judgments of the world around us.

Imagine that when you and I meet for the first time, we only have two minutes to spend together. For the first minute, our conversation is delightful and you feel warmly accepted by me. But during the second minute, I scream at you and chase you around the room with a large knife. What is the overall effect? Do you remember only our first minute together and feel loved and safe with me? Of course not. The effect of fear and pain are overwhelming. Until a child — or adult — is utterly convinced that they're loved unconditionally, only a small amount of fear is sufficient to destroy the effect of many moments of acceptance and safety.

Again, we must remember that the reason we were not loved unconditionally by our parents and others is that they were empty and afraid themselves. They were so occupied with their own needs and fears that they *could not* genuinely care about our happiness. With all their hearts, they tried to love us, but they had little or nothing to give. We then raise children of our own, unable to give them Real Love, either. And so it continues, generation after generation, until we learn how to change it.

Chapter Summary

Without Real Love, we feel a painful emptiness that we cannot tolerate.

To protect ourselves, we use Protecting Behaviors: lying, attacking, acting like victims, and running.

To fill our emptiness, we use Getting Behaviors: lying, attacking, acting like victims, and clinging.

With these unconscious behaviors, we get Imitation Love, which feels good for a moment but always fails to produce genuine happiness.

Chapter 5

Real Love
vs.
Imitation Love

If we don't learn the difference between Real and Imitation Love, we can easily be deceived and satisfied by the temporary pleasures of Imitation Love. That distraction can utterly prevent us from finding the Real Love that makes life worth living. That is the real danger of Imitation Love, that it seductively leads us away from the true source of happiness.

The best way to become familiar with Real Love, and to keep from confusing it with its many imitations, is to simply *feel it* consistently. Chapters 7-11 describe how we can do that. Fortunately, before we've acquired this familiarity, we can look for two characteristics which reliably distinguish Real Love from Imitation Love: (1) the absence of Getting and Protecting Behaviors; and (2) the absence of disappointment, anger, and fear.

1. The Absence of Getting and Protecting Behaviors
— Real Love is Freely Given and Received —

It's Real Love when someone cares about *my* happiness without any concern for what *they* might get. It's Real Love when I care about someone else's happiness with no thought for my own reward. Real Love is always a gift freely given and freely received. It's a genuine caring that cannot be manipulated, traded, or forced. When we do *anything* to get people to like us (Getting Behaviors) or to hurt us less (Protecting Behaviors), what we receive is not freely offered and can only be Imitation Love.

Without Real Love, it's natural that we manipulate people to get attention, praise, and power. We briefly feel better when we get those things, but the moment we reach out in any way to get something from another person, we ruin any possibility of receiving a true gift from them.

Imagine that you see me walking toward your house with a bushel of apples. Eager to have some for yourself, you hurry out and say to me: "I haven't had a bite to eat all day (**lie**), and nobody will give me anything (**victim**)."

Me: "But . . ."

You: (interrupting me) "And I hope you remember all the things I've done for you in the past (**attacking** me with guilt)."

I then give you the apples without you knowing that I had picked them for *you* and was bringing them to you as a gift.

Now imagine a different scene, where I suddenly appear in your doorway with a bushel of apples and say, "I picked these for you, and I hope you enjoy them." You had no expectation that I was coming, and it's clear from my behavior that I expect nothing from you in return.

Although you received the apples in both scenes, you felt very differently about them on each occasion. In the first scene, you lied, acted like a victim, and attacked me (Getting Behaviors) before I could offer you my gift. The apples still tasted good, but you could not *feel loved* because you know that *you manipulated me* to get them. Real Love can only be felt when it's freely offered *and* freely received. Although I offered my gift freely, you did not receive it freely.

In effect, you *bought* the apples with your behavior — by acting like a victim and attacking me — just like you'd paid for them with money. Because of what you did, what I gave you could not *feel* like a gift. In the second scene, however, you were touched by my gift, which was freely given and received.

When we do *anything* to manipulate attention, approval, praise, sex, etc. from another person, whatever they give us can't feel like a gift, and we will not feel loved. When we receive something after manipulating someone for it, we can only feel as though we *paid* for it with our manipulation. Even when a gift *is* freely given to us, it *feels* purchased when we use Getting and Protecting Behaviors. With manipulation, we transform any possibility of Real Love into Imitation Love, like turning gold into lead. Most of us have been lying, attacking, and running — filling our lives with Imitation Love — for so long that we don't even recognize when we do those things.

Lying

When we say or do anything to get someone to like us without revealing our intent, we're lying. It's often done unconsciously, but it's still lying. And when we lie, we can only get Imitation Love. The other person can't see or love *us*, only our deception. Even in the rare situation where they can see through our lies and genuinely love us, our knowledge that we've lied to them makes it impossible for us to *feel* Real Love.

Attacking (and disappointment)

We never attack another person because we care about *their* happiness. We do it to get something for ourselves. Anger and criticism are common forms of attacking. It is impossible to care about the happiness of another person while we're angry at them. That single Getting and Protecting Behavior probably destroys more relationships than anything else.

Disappointment is more subtle than anger, but it's still a very powerful form of attack. When we feel disappointed, we're concerned about what *we* didn't get, not for the welfare of someone else. And we're accusing our partner of being defective for not satisfying our expectations. Every sigh and frown is filled with disappointment and accusation, and we feel that way so often we think it's normal.

We lie about the selfishness of our disappointment because we know the truth would make us look bad. We don't want to be seen as selfish and attacking, but until we tell the truth about this, we can't change the damage being caused by the attacks our partners always feel when we're disappointed.

If your partner completely ignored your birthday, would you be disappointed? Sure, and that's natural. But it's also selfish. Our disappointment reveals that we expect something for ourselves; we're not concerned primarily for the happiness of our partner. When your partner snaps at you, are you disappointed or offended? Almost everyone is, but it's still a selfish reaction. If we were truly loving, our only concern would be for *their* happiness, and there would be no disappointment or offense.

Acting like victims

We act like victims to protect ourselves and to selfishly get attention. We can't do that and simultaneously care about the happiness of someone else.

Running

For our own safety, we run away when we're in pain and afraid. When we do that, we can't give Real Love, nor can we feel it when it's given to us.

Clinging

How often have we heard the following expressions in movies, songs, and in our own lives:

"*I* can't live without you."
"You make *me* so happy."
"Please don't leave *me*."

We actually believe these are expressions of love. If we can't live without someone, that must be true love, right? No, it's just clinging. We're selfishly hanging on to someone and desperately sucking all the attention we can get from them. These are not expressions of love, but of *need*.

2. The Absence of Disappointment, Anger, and Fear

We can also distinguish Real and Imitation Love by how we *feel*. When we're disappointed, angry, or afraid, we can only be concerned for our own welfare, not the happiness of another person. We can only see what our partner might do *to* us or *for* us. In other words, when we're afraid or angry, feeling and giving Real Love are impossible.

There is great practical significance to this understanding. For example, if you're talking to your wife and feeling impatient (angry) with her, you *know* that you're not unconditionally loving her. You're either attacking her, or you will be very shortly. The solution is obvious: firmly press your upper and lower lips together and leave them in that position. Whatever you say while you're not loving can only hurt your relationship. Wait until you no longer feel angry before you continue the conversation, or even better, learn to take the steps necessary to find Real Love (Chapters 7-11) and bring to your relationship the one ingredient that can change everything.

An Example of Imitation Love
Revealing Itself

Without Real Love, we unconsciously manipulate our partners to give us relief from the pain of feeling empty and alone.

Lying

Frank enjoyed football, hated school, and avoided "sissy stuff" like dancing. When he met Diane, he'd been out of high school for several years and was working as a forklift operator at a carpet mill. He was immediately attracted to her and eager to please her.

Diane: "I love to dance. How about you?"

Frank answered that he did, which was not true. But he said what she wanted to hear. He set up a date to go dancing that weekend. On their first date, they talked about Diane's experiences in college and how much she enjoyed being with educated people.

Diane: "What kind of work do you do?"

Frank: "I'm a supervisor (lie) at a carpet plant, but I'm going back to school soon to finish my degree (lie)."

Frank wanted a relationship with Diane. She was beautiful, intelligent, and seemed to enjoy his company. All that made him feel good, and he wanted it to continue. But a relationship isn't a result of what we want; it's the natural result of the choices that two partners made long before they came together (Chapter 6). Frank didn't understand that. He thought he could fabricate a relationship with Diane by trying to be what she liked. Almost all of us do things like that in relationships, and the results are terrible.

There was nothing wrong with Frank driving a forklift, hating to dance, or being different than Diane in many ways. They could still have had a great relationship with those differences. The fatal flaw in their relationship was Frank's lies, his pretending to be someone that Diane would love and not criticize. He was not consciously aware that he was lying. He lied only because he'd never been unconditionally loved, and his subsequent emptiness and fear utterly controlled his behavior. He could not stop himself from trying to make her like him. He believed — as most of us do — that affection is earned, and that often means pretending to be what a potential partner likes.

Diane hadn't been unconditionally loved, either, and she hoped Frank would make her happy. She sensed Frank's lack of enthusiasm about school, and it was obvious he rarely danced, but she enjoyed feeling important when she made him happy, and she was flattered that he obviously tried hard to please her.

Attacking

Frank and Diane got married, and soon they became weary of trading Imitation Love. Lying is exhausting, and the effect of Imitation Love always wears off even when the lies are expertly told. Despite making many promises, Frank never went dancing again, nor did he go back to school. Understandably, Diane felt betrayed and was afraid she'd made a mistake in marrying Frank. Her initial reaction to fear was to lie, to act as though it didn't matter. But eventually her disappointment became unbearable, and she chose to attack.

Diane: "We never go dancing anymore (attack)."

Frank: "I work hard all day. When I get home, I'm too tired for that (lie)."

Diane: "You keep promising to take me (a lie Frank periodically told Diane to stop her nagging), but you never do. And you promise to go back to school, too, but you don't. You're just lazy (attack)."

Diane hoped she could force Frank to do what she wanted, in the hope that she would then feel loved. When she was angry, she did get his attention, and that felt better than being totally helpless and ignored. But that didn't last and it certainly wasn't love. Attacking never produces Real Love. When we insist on changing our partners, the result is fruitless and frustrating to everyone.

Acting like a victim

When lying and attacking failed to get Diane what she wanted, she unconsciously changed her approach. During one of their many arguments, she burst into tears.

Diane: "You never do anything with me anymore. I sit around the house miserable, and you just don't care."

Diane acted like a victim, hoping to get Frank's sympathy. It wasn't Real Love, but she did get him to listen, and that briefly felt better than being completely alone. Victims are always saying variations on the following:

"Look what you've done **to** me."
"Look what you should have done **for** me."
"It's not my fault."

Clinging

On the occasions when Frank gave in to the manipulating and did what Diane wanted, she was often effusively grateful and complimentary. By doing that, she hoped to make Frank feel like doing those things for her again. That's clinging.

When Frank didn't give her what she wanted — when he went out with his friends, for example — she used another form of clinging.

Diane: "Do you *have* to go out tonight? I really wish we could spend more time together."

With her gratitude, flattery, and begging, Diane was clinging to Frank, hoping to squeeze all the attention she could get from him. Clinging never produces Real Love.

Running

Eventually, all of their Getting and Protecting Behaviors failed to produce the love and happiness Diane and Frank wanted. So they protected themselves by simply avoiding each other. Eventually, they divorced, having learned nothing from their experiences together and certain to repeat their mistakes in the next relationship.

The Problem and the Solution

Diane and Frank did their very best to make their relationship work, but in the absence of Real Love, they could only watch each other drown. And then they each made the situation worse by using Getting and Protecting Behaviors. How frustrating it was for them to do everything they could and still fail miserably. That's why there's such heartbreak in failed relationships — when our very best efforts are unsuccessful, what hope is there?

Fortunately, we can all find Real Love. The supply is infinite. We can all find people capable of seeing us clearly and loving us (Chapters 7-11). Even better, we can all learn to become unconditionally loving ourselves (Chapters 14-17).

Chapter Summary

Real Love can be consistently distinguished from Imitation Love. There are no Getting and Protecting Behaviors in Real Love. There is also no disappointment, anger, or fear in Real Love.

Real Love is always freely given and received.

When we do anything to manipulate other people to give us what we want, whatever they give us becomes Imitation Love and is therefore worthless.

Chapter 6

The Truth About
Relationships

We can do a lot more to improve our relationships when we truly understand what a relationship is. **A relationship is the natural result of people making independent choices.**

"Independent Choices"

We need to discuss the two important phrases in the definition of a relationship. First "independent choices."

Everyone has the right to choose what they say and do.

That is the Law of Choice. It's the most fundamental principal of relationships. Nothing is more important than our ability to choose for ourselves. Imagine what our lives would be like if that were taken from us. We wouldn't be individuals at all, only tools in the hands of those who made our choices for us.

A painting is composed of countless individual brush strokes. Similarly, who we are is a result of all the choices we have made over a lifetime. Every decision has made us more alone or loved, angry or happy, weak or strong. In our infancy, other people applied those strokes to the canvas of our lives, but with time, we increasingly took the brush into our own hands. From all those choices, we've created a canvas with a unique color, which includes our personality and style, our needs and fears, and even our Getting and Protecting Behaviors.

"Natural Result"
— Mixing Colors —

When we mix blue and yellow paint, the natural result is green. Green isn't something we hope for or even work for. It just happens *every time* we mix blue and yellow. Similarly, relationships naturally result from the blending of the colors of each partner, colors produced by the choices each partner has made independently over a lifetime. If I'm yellow and you're blue, our relationship will be green. It doesn't matter that I *want* our relationship to be orange, or that you want it to be turquoise. The result **will be** green.

Our relationships are therefore often not what we expect or want them to be, just as expectations and desires are completely irrelevant when mixing two colors of paint. Relationships can only be the result of the *choices we've already made*. If two people have been unconditionally loved and have made a lifetime of unconditionally loving choices, they *will* have a mutually loving relationship. However, if they have not been unconditionally loved, they *will* choose to get Imitation Love and protect themselves, and the result of those choices in a relationship *cannot* be loving. It can only be the natural result of the interaction of all their Getting and Protecting Behaviors — and that is never happiness.

The Purpose of Relationships

As we talk about relationships, it's helpful to understand the only useful purpose of any relationship: receiving and giving Real Love. There is no greater joy than being loved and loving others. Nothing else comes close. Any relationship that doesn't contribute to feeling loved or loving others is a waste of time and happiness.

Choices

Joan was angry as she spoke about her husband Tyler to a wise friend. Remember that a wise man is anyone who feels sufficiently loved in a given moment that he or she can unconditionally accept and love another person (p. 22). I'll be using the term "wise man" a lot. We can all learn to find wise men and women for ourselves. They're everywhere, and we'll talk more about that in Chapter 10.

Joan: "The man lives like a pig. He throws his stuff all over the floor, and then I have to clean up after him. I've talked to him about it a million times, but he never listens."

Wise man: "So you want Tyler to be neater and more considerate of you. Is that right?"

Joan: "Yes."

Wise man: "Then your relationship is doomed. Relationships result from the choices people make independently. Tyler has chosen to be a pig, and he gets to make that choice, even if it's inconvenient for you. He's almost certainly been a pig all his life, long before he met you. But that doesn't make you a helpless victim here. You still have your own choice to make."

Joan: "What choice do I have?"

Wise man: "As I see it, you can make one of three:
              (1) live with the pig and like it;
              (2) live with the pig and hate it; or
              (3) leave the pig."

Joan: "But . . ."

Wise man: "There is no 'but.' You want a *fourth choice*, to stop him from being a pig. But that would violate Tyler's right to choose (p. 55). A world without choice would be a horrible place for everyone. You only get to make choices that involve *your* behavior, not his."

Most of us are like Joan. We're dissatisfied with our partners for many reasons, and we want to change them. But relationships are not determined by what we *want* from our partners. They're determined by the choices that we and our partners have already made independently.

THE FOUR CHOICES

We only have four choices to make with any partner. Let's deal with the fourth choice first, the one that Joan wanted to make — the one that we really don't get to make.

The Fourth and Worst Choice
— Change Our Partner —

We all like *some* things about our partners — that's why we started a relationship with them — but there are usually other things that we don't like about them. It seems natural that the solution would be to change the things we don't like. We do that when we rearrange the furniture or change the television channel — why not do it with people, too?

It's Selfish and
It's Not Real Love

Changing someone else to suit our needs is controlling, arrogant, selfish, manipulative, demanding, and destructive. Any effort on our part to control another person proves that we're interested in **our** happiness, not theirs. It's understandable that we want people to do things for us and that we never want them to inconvenience or hurt us. But when we use Getting and Protecting Behaviors to manipulate people to do what we want, we make Real Love impossible (pp. 45-7).

It's Very Difficult to Change People

Our partners have acquired their attitudes and behaviors from a lifetime of experience. They can't suddenly give all that up just because we want them to. But we continue to waste our lives trying. Joan worked very hard to get Tyler to be more neat in spite of the fact that her efforts to control him caused nothing but more contention in their relationship.

No Relationship

With enormous effort and persistence, it is possible to change some things about another person. Some of us attack people or play the victim so effectively that we really can get our partners to behave differently. But the victory is hollow. Anything we get as a result of manipulation cannot be Real Love and is therefore worthless.

A relationship is the natural result of the choices my partner and I make independently. If I control you in any way, you can't make independent choices, and I can no longer have a relationship with who *you* really are. For example, I interact with my shoes every day, but my shoes and I don't have a real relationship because my shoes don't make independent choices. They're controlled by me and are therefore nothing more than a part of myself. When I'm with my shoes, I'm only with myself—I'm still alone. When I control your choices, you become like my shoes. You're only an object and a part of me. And then I'm alone. *Controlling other people makes us alone.*

There were times when Joan's nagging and blaming were so unbearable that Tyler actually did clean up his mess. When that happened, Joan thought she was getting what she wanted, but what a price she paid! He resented her, and because his cooperation was not freely offered, she never felt loved. Everyone lost. Real Love can only be offered by an independent partner who is making their own choices. We can't get that from someone when we manipulate and control them.

Unloving

The worst consequence of controlling others is that we can't learn to be loving, which is the greatest joy of all. We can't be happy while we're selfishly manipulating people.

Expectations

Most of us would deny that we control the lives of our partners. And yet we do it every day. Certainly we don't lead our partners around in chains, but we do control them in many other ways. All of our Getting and Protecting Behaviors are intended to manipulate people to get what we want from them. And when our partners fail to do what we want — when we can't *control* them — we uniformly become disappointed and angry, don't we?

When we don't feel unconditionally loved, we feel so empty that we unavoidably cling desperately to any partner who gives us any attention at all. The more we get from them, the more we *expect* from them. Our relationships often fail because we choose to burden our partners with expectations they can't possibly satisfy.

Sometimes we justify our expectations because we've given something — our time and attention, for example — to the person we have expectations of. In other words, we think we have the right to expect something because we've *paid* for it. Sadly, that leads to the condition that exists in most relationships: "I'll give you what you want if you give me what I want." It's a trading of Imitation Love. That may satisfy both partners temporarily, but no relationship can be genuinely fulfilling when it's based on trading rather than unconditional giving.

We never have the right to expect that another person will do anything for us. I suggest that you read that sentence again. If we understood and remembered that one principle, there would be no conflict on the face of the planet. It naturally follows from the Law of

Choice. If I truly allow you to make your own choices, which is obvious if you are to remain an independent human being, what right do I ever have to expect you to do *anything*? How incredibly arrogant it is for me to ever expect you to change who you are to make my life more convenient in any way! And yet we do that all the time. We expect our spouses to love us, even when they don't have the love to give. We expect our children to love us, when it's our responsibility to love them. We expect other drivers on the road to make us the center of the universe and do whatever it takes to make our lives easier. We expect our employers to ignore everything else in their lives and make our happiness their first priority. And so on.

Every time we're disappointed or angry at someone, we declare our expectation that people should give up their right to make their own choices and should choose instead to make us happy. *And we don't have the right to do that*. We don't have the right to violate the law of choice for our convenience. Expectations are selfish and unloving, and are therefore *wrong* (pp. 24-5).

1. The Happy Choice
— Live With It and Like It —

Tyler's messiness was just one brush stroke of thousands that combined to create his own beautiful color. Instead of choosing to accept and enjoy the beauty of his overall canvas, Joan chose to be miserably distracted by the one stroke that inconvenienced her. And, as is the case in nearly all relationships, there were some other things that bothered her, too.

Real Love is what we all really want from every relationship. We only insist on changing and controlling our partners because we don't know any better — because we've never seen Real Love and don't know how to get it. As we feel unconditionally loved, we begin to see people without the blinding effects of emptiness and fear (p. 43). And then every human being becomes beautiful to us and easy to accept. It really happens that way. It is the purpose of this book to make it easier for us to learn how to see, accept, and love our partners (Chapters 14-17). That is where real happiness is found.

2. The Angry Choice
— Live With It and Hate It —

Many of us have tried to change a partner so many times that we've finally quit trying. We stay in the relationship, but we continue to wish that our partner was different, and we resent them when they're not. In effect, we choose to stay in a relationship where unhappiness is the only possibility. What a foolish choice.

If I'm blue and you're yellow, our relationship will be green. Green is a beautiful color, but I will entirely fail to enjoy it if I expect another color instead. When we want our partner to be different than they are, we *choose* to be unhappy.

3. The Final Choice
— Leave It —

If we don't like the color of a painting, we can simply leave the room. That's the approach we take when we abandon a relationship, emotionally or physically. There are two ways to do this, blaming and not.

Blaming

When we leave a relationship and blame our unhappiness on our partner, we use all the Getting and Protecting Behaviors:

lying — believing and saying that our partner is at fault, when the real cause of our misery is the long-standing lack of Real Love in *our* lives and *our* inability to accept and love our partner

attacking — assaulting our partner with criticism and accusations acting like a victim — "look what he (or she) has done to me!"

running

We learn nothing when we blame our partners, nor can we be happy.

Not Blaming

When we're just learning to tell the truth and feel loved, some people are so confusing or threatening to us that we simply can't be around them without feeling empty and afraid, and then we unavoidably return to the familiar use of Getting and Protecting Behaviors. It may be unwise to spend our time with such people, but we need to admit that **we** are the problem. *We* are not loving enough to participate in a loving relationship with them.

In short, leaving a relationship can be the right thing to do, but we can do that without blaming our partners for our decision. Leaving relationships is the subject of Chapter 27 and is not a decision to make lightly.

Making a Choice

Joan and her friend continued their conversation from p. 57.

Joan: "But I only want Tyler to . . ."

Wise man: "As we've discussed, you can't make yourself happy by changing Tyler. Haven't you proven that over and over? In all the times that you've nagged and whined at him, have you ever changed him or made yourself happy?"

Joan: "Well . . . no."

Wise man: "Then let's look at some other choices."

Joan's friend then talked to her about how relationships change when both partners have Real Love in their lives (Chapters 7-11).

Trying to change people (the fourth choice) or resenting them (choice #2) only guarantees our unhappiness. How insane we are to keep doing those things! Only two of the four choices above really make any sense. We can (a) stay with a relationship and learn how to love and be loved; or (b) we can leave it. I re-state my emphasis that leaving is rarely the best choice, at least initially.

Telling the Truth About OUR Relationships

It's critical that we see the truth about the condition of the relationships we have now. Only then can we do something about them. Joan's friend helped her do some of that above.

"I Love You"

As with all people in a relationship with conflict, Joan was puzzled: "I don't understand this. When we first met, I loved him so much. And he made me so happy." The truth is she never did truly love him. Early in their relationship, each time Joan said, "I love you," what she really meant was this:

> "I like how you make me feel. I've been lonely for a long time and looking for someone to make me happy — and you're what I've been looking for. I love the attention you give me. I like the excitement of being touched by you. I like the praise and envy I get from other people when they see me with you. When I'm with you, I feel less alone, more important, and more alive."

Joan didn't love Tyler. She *needed* him. She liked it when he gave her what she wanted. And in the first few months of their relationship, he devoted all his energy to her and succeeded in making her feel less empty and alone. Because of his efforts, she sincerely believed that she'd found true happiness. But on increasingly frequent occasions, Tyler failed to satisfy all of Joan's demands. Either he didn't do exactly what she wanted, or — more frequently — what he did wasn't as exciting or fulfilling as it used to be. Nearly all couples experience this as they notice that kissing, holding hands, having sex, talking, and so on aren't nearly as exciting the thousandth time as they were the first time. Joan gradually became dissatisfied with what she was getting from Tyler, and she blamed him for that.

We're afraid to closely examine what we call "love." We want love to be magical and romantic, which really means irresponsible. We want love to rescue us from all our problems with no effort on our part. The pattern of "falling in love" goes like this:

1. We feel alone and want someone to make us happy.

2. We find someone with qualities we like, and if they share those with us, we feel wonderful and say that we "love" that partner.

3. We then do our best to make our partner feel good, too. We do this mostly — and unconsciously — so they'll keep giving us what we want. When we succeed in pleasing our partner, they naturally say that they "love" us, too.

4. Inevitably, one of us fails to make the other sufficiently happy, and that is followed by disappointment, resentment, demands, and anger.

5. We may then choose to continue in an unhappy relationship — often for a lifetime — or we may look for someone else to make us happy, starting the pattern all over again.

Until we're honest about what we call love, we condemn ourselves to endlessly repeat the frustrating and destructive pattern of falling in and out of "love."

"I Love You Because . . ."

A couple in love often says things like, "I love you because . . ." And then they describe things about their partner that they like. We enjoy hearing those things about ourselves. We like hearing that we're witty, handsome, beautiful, and intelligent. We feel flattered and important when someone says nice things about us. But those statements are also the beginning of the end of the relationship.

If I love you **because** of something you do, you're now obligated to continue doing that thing if you want to keep my affection. If you stop doing it, the reason I stated for loving you is obviously gone — at least partially. When we say why we like someone, we're unconsciously expressing an expectation or demand for what we want to keep receiving from that person. We don't mean to do any of this, but we still do it, and it destroys our relationships. Expectations invariably lead to disappointment and unhappiness.

Other Relationships

Unconsciously, we expect all our partners — friends, parents, children, siblings, co-workers, and neighbors — to make us happier. There's an element of "falling in love" in all those relationships. We "love" the people who make us feel good, and we dislike the people who fail to make us happy or actually do things to inconvenience or hurt us.

When We Tell the Truth About Ourselves, We Discover What Relationships Really Are

The Wart King (pp. 19-22) tried to control his relationship with everyone in the kingdom, and as a result, he was alone and miserable. Initially, he tried to control his relationship with the Wise Man, too, and again the consequences were unhappy. But when he told the truth about himself and stopped controlling the behavior of the Wise Man, a natural and genuine relationship developed, and he was no longer alone.

For most of my life, I tried to change the people around me for my convenience. I required them to give me what I wanted instead of enjoying what they had to offer. When I finally admitted that, I was able to do something about it. Over a period of years, I learned how to find Real Love for myself (Chapter 7). As unconditional love eliminated my emptiness and fear, I saw people more clearly and appreciated the beauty in them. It was then easy to accept them, love them, and develop mutually fulfilling relationships with them. We can all learn to do the same.

Chapter Summary

A relationship is the natural result of people making independent choices.

After our partners have made their own choices, we have four choices available to us:
1. Live with them and like it.
2. Live with them and hate it.
3. Leave them.
4. Try to change them.

We never have the right to expect that another person will do anything for us.

When we feel unconditionally loved ourselves and learn to accept our partner's choices, we can enjoy any relationship.

Finding Real Love

Chapter 7

Finding Love

"With Real Love, nothing else matters. Without it, nothing else is enough." (p. 10) There is nothing in the world that begins to compare with the joy of feeling loved and loving others. Fortunately, finding the unconditional love we need is easy if we consistently follow these simple steps:

1. Have a desire to change.
2. Exercise the faith that change is possible.
3. Tell the truth about ourselves.
4. Give up our Getting and Protecting Behaviors.

We'll discuss these steps individually in the next four chapters.

This process has been throughly tested. It works. Thousands of people have taken these steps and have filled their lives with Real Love. As a result, they have found a personal happiness and a joy in their relationships they never imagined possible.

The Wart King (pp. 19-22) was miserable as long as he hid his warts (lying), felt sorry for himself (victim), and tried to control the people around him (attacking). He only found real happiness when he took the same steps to find love that all of us must take.

1. After many years of being lonely and unhappy, he finally decided that he didn't want to live like that anymore. When he heard about

the existence of The Wise Man, he made the decision to do something different with his life and made the trek to see the old man on the mountain.

2. The Wart King had been laughed at all his life. It took considerable faith for him to leave his room and visit the Wise Man. When the old man confronted him with the truth about his warts, the king's faith was overwhelmed and he responded with all the Protecting Behaviors. But after experiencing once again the futility of those old responses, he summoned additional faith in what the Wise Man was doing and listened to what he said.

3. The turning point in the Wart King's journey to the mountain was when he took the step of not only listening to the Wise Man, but telling the truth about his own warts. It was only then that he truly began to feel the acceptance offered by the old man.

4. Although the Wart King did lash out with Protecting Behaviors at the beginning of their interaction, he eventually trusted The Wise Man enough to lay aside those behaviors and allow himself to experience the love given to him. Had the Wart King continued lying, attacking, acting like a victim, and running, he would have gained nothing from his visit to the mountain.

How Real Love Comes

In the beginning of our search, we don't usually find Real Love by the truckload. We feel it in small doses, a cupful here and there. In addition, Real Love doesn't come in the form of a romantic explosion or the playing of a brass band, contrary to what we see in movies and have come to expect in our own lives. Initially, it's like the song of a distant bird, soft and lovely. It may take time and experience for us to hear that quiet song, and we'll miss it entirely if we're listening for the brass band.

Don't be discouraged when you don't feel a tidal wave of love as you take the first steps toward finding it. You'll experience small moments of acceptance that will increase as you continue to tell the truth about yourself to people who are capable of seeing you. At times, you'll be afraid and will go back to getting Imitation Love and protecting yourself. In those moments, you'll lose the feeling of being loved for a while. Don't give up. Keep taking the steps (Chapters 8-11), and the feeling will come back.

The Reward

As we feel unconditionally loved, we begin to experience the kind of happiness defined on p. 10, a profound joy that most of us have never known. Real Love changes the way we see everything. It satisfies our greatest need and eliminates our greatest fear. Real Love is the most valuable prize of all. No effort to find it is too great.

Chapter 8

A Desire to Change

We can only become loving and happy if we have a genuine desire to learn and grow. But what we *say* means little or nothing — the truth is in our behavior. I can easily say that I want to win the gold medal for the 400-meter free-style swimming event in the upcoming Olympics, but then if I swim for only an hour a week and spend the rest of my time eating potato chips while watching television on the couch, it's quite clear that I don't *really* want to win the medal — isn't it?

What we have now, and what we'll have at the end of our lives, is the natural result of what we genuinely want. It's therefore important that we choose the things we want wisely, or we'll spend a lifetime pursuing and getting the things that can't possibly make us happy.

The Wrong Desire: Controlling Other People

When I talk to people who are unhappy with a relationship, they almost invariably say something like this about their partner: "I wish he (or she) would . . ." When our desire is to change or control our partner, happiness is never the result. We talked about that on pp. 58-61. Sadly, that's still what we usually try to do.

Healthy Desires

The only thing we can productively want to change in a relationship is ourselves.

Telling the truth about ourselves

It's good to have a desire to tell the truth about ourselves, a choice that doesn't violate the rights of others. When we tell the truth (Chapter 10), we start the process of feeling loved and loving others: Truth → Seen → Accepted → Loved (p. 22).

The desire to be happy

We can want — even expect — to be happy. The supply of joy is infinite. However, *it's always unhealthy to expect any of our happiness to come from a particular person or group of people.* That violates their freedom of choice. Unfortunately, we tend to do exactly that. When we find someone who makes us feel good, we do expect them to keep making us feel good — and that guarantees conflicts and unhappiness in a relationship.

A relationship is a natural result of people making independent decisions (p. 55). A *good* relationship is only possible when we *accept* the independent decisions of our partner. *We experience a beautiful freedom when we stop trying to get a specific person to make us happy* — or to give us anything at all. It's so much easier — and more productive — to simply be truthful about ourselves and allow people to *determine for themselves* how they want to interact with us, if at all. When we do that, anything they give us is then *real.* It's genuine and freely offered (Real Love), instead of forced and manipulated (Imitation Love). The instant we try in any way to get approval or affection from someone, we've paid for it, and we will not feel truly loved (pp. 45-7).

Wanting other people to be happy

We can want other people to be happy and to contribute to their happiness. That's the definition of Real Love. However, we cannot insist that they accept our efforts, no matter how much we think we have to offer them.

Killing the Desire to Change

If we don't have a strong desire to change our lives, we won't change. In physics, this is called inertia. Any object moving in a certain direction will tend to stay moving in that direction unless something changes its course. It's the same with us. We don't get wiser, stronger, and happier by accident. We must want to change and then do something about it. It's therefore wise to identify the things that destroy our desire to change, because those things guarantee our stagnation and unhappiness.

Imitation Love

When an addict gets enough of his drug, he calls that happiness and never addresses the real problems in his life, the problems that led to his drug use in the first place. That superficial satisfaction is therefore fatal. People with enough Imitation Love also think they're happy, and then they ignore what they really need to be genuinely happy. They see no reason to take the risk of telling the truth and doing the other things necessary to find Real Love (Chapters 9-11). The deception kills them. All forms of Imitation Love are highly addictive and deceptive, just like cigarettes or cocaine.

Being Right

The need to be right is a deadly enemy of growth and happiness.

Jane was miserable, and her marriage was falling apart. She spoke to a wise friend and presented a pile of evidence that all her misery was her husband's fault.

Wise woman: "What are **you** willing to do to change your relationship?"

Jane: "I'd do anything to not feel like this."

Wise woman: "Then tell me how all the problems in your marriage are
        your fault."

Jane couldn't do that, even after her friend helped her see that
Jane was empty, afraid, and using all the Getting and Protecting Behaviors as she interacted with her husband. Despite her claim that she
was willing to do anything to change her relationship, Jane was not
willing to admit that she was wrong. It was too important to her to be
right.

When we're unhappy in a relationship, we're always wrong.
When we're unhappy, we always use Getting and Protecting Behaviors, and those are behaviors that we *choose,* which means *we* are
responsible. Our unhappiness is never the fault of our partner. We're
not helpless babies anymore. We cannot insist on being right and at
the same time be sincere about trying to change our lives. For many of
us, it's helpful to understand that being wrong doesn't make us bad.
It's just the critical first step in telling the truth and finding Real Love in
relationships.

Some people seem to find it impossible to admit being wrong.
Being right is a protective habit they will not give up. Such people are
not evil — just afraid and angry. They've become so familiar with
Getting and Protecting Behaviors — being right is a combination of
lying and attacking — that they're terrified to do anything different.
However, even though their emptiness began in childhood, through no
fault of theirs, what they do about it now is *their* responsibility. We
are all responsible for the next step we take in our lives.

To those who can't seem to stop being right, I suggest this: when
you're unhappy, *something* is obviously not working. You *may be*
partly right about a situation in question, but *so what!?* Would you
rather be right or happy? The only worthwhile goal in life is to find joy.
If what we're doing isn't giving us joy, let's change it, even if we can
find some tiny thing we're doing that's blameless. Being right is worthless. Being happy is everything.

The Power of Wanting

If you genuinely want to feel loved and happy, and if you do what it takes to achieve that condition (Chapters 9-11), there is no force on earth that can stop you. It doesn't matter how many mistakes you've made, or how many people stand in your way. If you really want your life to change, you will succeed.

Chapter Summary

We do what we want to do, so it's important to want the right things if we want to be happy.

Wanting other people to change will never bring us happiness. Only changing ourselves will make us happy.

The desire to change ourselves is destroyed by Imitation Love and the need to be right.

Chapter 9

Faith

Like the Wart King, most of us have been hiding who we really are all our lives — and understandably so. We've learned from extensive experience that when people have seen our mistakes and flaws — our warts — they've painfully criticized us and withdrawn from us. We've responded with all the Getting and Protecting Behaviors, which have only kept us more alone and unhappy.

Why then do we keep using these behaviors which obviously don't work? Why don't we just stop and do something different? Because we can only do what we know. Unfortunately, as we learn about new things that *will* make us happier — like the principles in this book — we still tend to do the same old, ineffective things. We do that because the unknown scares us to death. We prefer to do what's *familiar* to us, even if it works poorly, rather than step out into the unknown where we could look stupid and feel lost. That approach isn't very smart, but fear has long made a mockery of wisdom.

Faith is the act of consciously choosing to experience what we don't know. That exposes us to possible danger, but it also creates the opportunity to learn and grow. Only with faith can we find Real Love and genuine happiness.

Faith is much more than words. Faith means believing that something is true and then *acting* on that belief, despite our fears. It's easy to stand on the ground and express a belief in the safety of sky diving.

When we actually jump out of a plane at 10,000 feet, that's faith. Similarly, it's easy to talk about wanting to change our lives, but we have no faith until we actually tell the truth about ourselves as the Wart King did — especially when people might criticize and reject us. We'll talk about that in Chapter 10.

Faith That Change is Possible

Most of us have searched earnestly for genuine happiness all our lives. But despite our best efforts with Imitation Love, we've failed. When we've done everything we know and nothing has worked, what's next? That's very discouraging. After all that failure, it takes enormous faith to once again pick ourselves up and believe that we can find Real Love and happiness. Without that faith, however, we'll never take the risks or expend the effort required to tell the truth about ourselves. And then we're doomed to continue feeling unloved and alone.

Faith in the Truth

Truth → Seen → Accepted → Loved (p. 22).

We can't feel loved until we tell the truth about ourselves, as the Wart King did. If we lie — to protect ourselves or to earn approval — other people can only see our lies, and then we can't experience the feeling that they truly see and love *us* as we really are. We can only believe that they love the lies we tell. We can't *feel* loved if we manipulate people in any way (pp. 45-7).

In the past, when people learned the truth about our mistakes and weaknesses, they often laughed at us, criticized us, punished us, and avoided us. We reacted by learning that when we lied, we often avoided the pain of criticism and rejection. It worked for us as children, so understandably, we continue to lie as adults. In addition, we tend to lie because that's what we've seen everyone else do. We've had few, if any, examples of people being consistently truthful about themselves.

After all those negative experiences with the truth, we naturally believe the same unpleasant affair will occur each time our flaws are exposed. That's why it takes faith to tell the truth about ourselves now. Having faith in the truth means being honest about ourselves even though we don't know what the results will be. It means continuing to tell the truth even when we're not certain we're being accepted. Faith means simply telling the truth and then waiting to see what happens. As we have the courage to do that, we will find the greatest gift of all, which is unconditional love and genuine happiness.

If we're physically out of shape, achieving fitness takes time and effort. We rarely feel a significant change in our overall well-being the first time we exercise. Similarly, the first time we tell the truth about ourselves, we may not feel a positive result. Without faith in the truth, we'll give up after any unsatisfying experience with the truth. We won't be honest about ourselves long enough to see the positive effect that always follows — because it follows after a period of time we can't predict. Without faith, we become frightened at the first sign of criticism or discomfort and go back to lying and using the other Getting and Protecting Behaviors. If we want to feel unconditional love, we must have faith and simply decide to keep telling the truth even when we're not getting the immediate results we expected.

Faith in Finding Real Love

Real Love is infinitely available. As we continue to tell the truth about ourselves, and as we avoid lying and using the other Getting and Protecting Behaviors, we *will* find people who are capable of loving us. Sometimes that only happens for moments at a time — and perhaps more slowly than we'd prefer — but if we're not defending ourselves, we'll feel those moments, and they will change our lives.

Sometimes people *will* attack us when we tell the truth about ourselves. Those people are just afraid and protecting themselves. Having faith in Real Love does not mean believing that we'll be loved by every person we meet, because many people are simply incapable of loving us at the moment we choose. Faith means believing that when we consistently tell the truth, *someone* will accept and love us — and they will. I've seen this confirmed too many times to ever doubt it again.

As we exercise this faith and feel the unconditional love that's available to all of us, we no longer have to insist that any particular person love us right now. If the next ten people I meet fail to accept me — even if they're critical and otherwise attacking — that doesn't bother me at all, because I have faith that other people *will* love me. And I have plenty of actual experiences where people *have* loved me. It doesn't matter how many people don't love us, only that some people do. With faith, remembering that *one* person loves us can outweigh the effect of a thousand people criticizing us.

Faith in Human Nature

Without Real Love, we're blinded by our needs and fears. We can't see who people really are. We only see what they can do **for** us or **to** us. Empty and afraid, we naturally expect some relief from the people around us — how could they see our obvious distress and not offer to help us? We reason to ourselves that when someone doesn't help us — or worse, they inconvenience or attack us — they must be hurting us intentionally and therefore must be "bad."

When we believe people are bad, we fear them, use them, and protect ourselves from them. That makes them — and us — feel even more empty and afraid. And then we all use more Getting and Protecting Behaviors. It's impossible to have loving relationships with people when we see them in that way.

With love and understanding, we begin to see that people only do "bad" things — which are all Getting and Protecting Behaviors — when they feel unloved and afraid. People are not inherently evil, just desperate because they're drowning (pp. 11-15). In that condition, they can't help us; all they can do is defend themselves and try to satisfy their own needs. When people are sufficiently loved, they lose their need to use Getting and Protecting Behaviors. When we understand and believe that, we stop judging people as bad, after which accepting and loving them is easy. With faith in the basic goodness of people, loving relationships become infinitely easier.

Faith That People Do Their Best

I don't know anyone who would eat with pigs out of a trough in a muddy barnyard if they knew that a well-prepared meal was available on a table in a clean house — do you? And that's because *we really do make the best choice we can see.*

One of the choices we make is whether we'll be loving and happy or doubting and miserable, and in that area we also tend to make the best choice we can see. When we're not being loving, we simply don't see the availability of that choice. We haven't been taught *how* to be loving. We're incapable of doing what we've never been taught and can't give what we've never received.

The same is true of everyone else. When other people inconvenience us or get angry at us, they're just empty and afraid and protecting themselves. They can't give what *they* never received, either. But we get angry at people when they treat *us* badly, don't we? We treat them as though they are somehow intentionally withholding something from us. We actually believe that other people choose to hurt us when they could just as easily choose to love us. That is never the case.

If you have any doubt that emptiness and fear are the cause of anger, the next time someone is angry at you — preferably someone you've known for a while — give them a big hug, apologize for inconveniencing them, and tell them you love them. But only if you mean it. As their emptiness and fear disappear, see how long their anger lasts. They're only protecting themselves with their anger, and doing what they've seen everyone around them do in similar situations. That doesn't justify what they do, but it does explain it.

People who are angry at us are doing their best and simply *can't* love us as we'd like. They're doing all they can do. I've never met an angry person who was intentionally withholding a secret supply of love. When we understand that, it makes no sense for us to resent angry people anymore. And then it's much easier to have faith in them and have a loving relationship with them.

Faith in Our Partner

"Trust is earned." We've all heard this spoken many times, usually in an accusing way to someone whose trustworthiness is in doubt. This commonly-accepted phrase clearly demonstrates the destructive lack of faith we have in each other. And it's a deadly lie that we use to hide our fear and anger. When people say, "Trust is earned," what they really mean is this:

"I'm empty and afraid. I've been used and hurt by people many times in the past, and I'm afraid that everyone I meet will do the same things to me. I therefore protect myself constantly until people individually *prove* that I don't need to be afraid of them."

That faithless and frightened view of the world guarantees that we'll use Protecting Behaviors, which only leads to everyone feeling more afraid, unloved, and alone.

When we require people to prove that they're worth trusting, we naturally — and mostly unconsciously — look for evidence that they're *not* trustworthy. That's understandable, since we're afraid of being hurt and eager to protect ourselves. However, the consequences of that fearful and protective approach are terribly destructive to relationships and to our own happiness:

1. We find the slightest mistakes to justify our fears and prove that our suspicions were correct. But as people learn to tell the truth and become loving, they *will* make mistakes. They have to. When we feel unloved and empty, and when we have no faith in people, we see every mistake as a threat to our well-being. That outlook keeps us afraid of almost everyone we know, which makes loving relationships impossible.

2. We see mistakes where they don't exist. In the absence of Real Love, we see the potential for being hurt everywhere, even with people who are quite harmless. We tend to see what we're looking for.

As long as we assume that our partners are hurtful, they can never prove otherwise because we will interpret everything they do in a negative way, confirming our critical assumptions about them. We do all this to protect ourselves, but ironically, it only succeeds in hurting us. The more we protect ourselves, the more alone we feel. We can't feel accepted and loved by people we fear. Loving relationships become much easier when we simply choose to have faith and trust people. Waiting for other people to change and make us feel safe is slow, lazy, and irresponsible.

Before they were married, Ellen and Chris fell in love like most couples. Neither of them had been unconditionally loved, so they were thrilled with all the attention and acceptance they got from each other. They were certain that their love was genuine, but without prior experience with Real Love, they could only trade Imitation Love. When the excitement of approval, praise, and sex began to wear off, as it always does, they became increasingly dissatisfied with each other.

Chris started to avoid Ellen (running), while Ellen demanded that Chris give her the attention he used to when they were dating (victim, attacking). Desperate to do something, Ellen invited a friend to help them, a man who had always been accepting and loving with each of them in the past. Remember, a wise man is anyone who feels loved enough that they can clearly see and accept another person.

Ellen: "We never talk anymore. We never do anything together."

Chris: "Why would I want to? You're angry and nag at me all the time."

Ellen: (instantly angry) "And you don't ever listen to me or spend time with me. If I don't get angry, I can't get you to do anything."

Chris: "See? That's what I mean. You're angry right now, and I hate talking to you when you're like that. Who wouldn't hate it?"

Chris and Ellen argued a little longer, each intent on proving that the other was at fault.

Wise man: "Chris, it's clear that you do avoid Ellen. And I understand that. Ellen, you're obviously angry at Chris, probably even more when you're alone than here with me watching. And I understand that, too. But at this point we don't need to go over all the mistakes you've made. It's not helpful. The important question is this: are you both willing to try something different that will change your relationship completely?"

Chris and Ellen immediately sensed that their friend had no interest in criticizing them. They *felt* his acceptance and desire to help them. That is the effect that a wise man has on people.

The wise man explained that neither of them felt unconditionally loved, and they each saw that was true. All their lives, the pain of feeling unloved and empty had dictated their unproductive use of Getting and Protecting Behaviors. In the beginning of their relationship, they understandably hoped that their partner would give them the happiness they didn't have. But without Real Love, they could only give each other Imitation Love, which never lasts. The wise man explained the process of learning to tell the truth about themselves and creating opportunities for people to accept them unconditionally. He also gave them the names of some people who were capable of loving them in that way, and he suggested that they contact those people every day. They met again a week later.

Wise man: "What have you learned in the past week?"

Ellen: "Nothing's changed. He still doesn't do anything with me."

Wise man: "Did either of you talk to any of the people I recommended?"

Chris had talked to several people, and as he told them the truth about his mistakes and fears, he felt accepted. He enjoyed that so much, he even had dinner with two of the men he spoke with on the phone. This was a new and exciting experience for him. He then tried to tell the truth about himself to Ellen, but those conversations went poorly. Ellen had not made any phone calls, nor had she met with any of the people the wise man had recommended.

Wise man: "I'm happy for you, Chris. It sounds like you had a good time."

Ellen: "But he hasn't changed. He still avoids me all the time."

Wise man: "Ellen, Chris is trying something very different for him. He's trying to tell the truth about himself. Because he's just starting, he still makes lots of mistakes, especially with you.

That's unavoidable as he learns to be truthful and loving."

"Now let's talk about you. What are *you* willing to do to have a better relationship with Chris?"

Ellen: "How can I do anything when *he* . . ."

Wise man: "We've already talked about Chris. He's taking the first steps toward changing his life. That's all he can do right now. But now we're talking about you. Until **you** make the decision to have faith in Chris and trust that he's doing his best to learn to tell the truth and love you — no matter how many mistakes he makes — your relationship with him can't go anywhere."

Ellen: "Me?! You're saying it's **my** fault?"

Wise man: "I didn't say anything about fault. Placing blame is useless. I'm talking about how *you* can move forward, be happier, and change your relationship."

Ellen: "How can I have faith in him when he still avoids me and doesn't care about me?"

Wise man: "That's why it's called faith. Faith means acting on a belief that doesn't yet have proof. If Chris has to *prove* that he's completely truthful and loving before you believe it and accept him, you'll never have a loving relationship with him. You'll never see the real changes in him, and he won't want to share them with you. You'll never really trust him until you simply choose to do so."

Ellen: "You're suggesting that I trust him even when he's avoiding me and being angry at me?"

Wise man: "Yes. Real faith means believing that he's doing his best to tell the truth and love you even when there are times that it appears he's not. Until you're willing to do that, your relationship will not change. Trust is *not* earned; it's given, like a gift."

Ellen could not accept what the wise man said, but Chris did. He *chose* to have faith in people, and that decision changed his life. He continued to tell the truth about himself to several wise men and women, and he trusted them to love him. As he felt seen, accepted, and loved, he felt less needy and afraid. He began to experience a consistent happiness that replaced the fear and anger that had consumed him in the past. Seeing clearly, he found it easier to accept Ellen and care about her happiness (Real Love).

Ellen chose to keep insisting that "trust is earned." She never did tell the truth about her own mistakes and fears, and she remained alone and miserable.

A lack of faith in other people keeps us in a constant state of doubt, fear, and protecting ourselves. And then loving relationships are impossible.

Make a Choice

Faith is not a feeling. It's not wishing or hoping. It's a choice we make. With faith, we **choose** to believe something is true and then **behave** as though it were. Anything short of that is not faith and will not lead to growth or happy relationships.

Chris chose to believe that people were doing their best as they learned to tell the truth about themselves and as they learned to see and accept him. As a result, he enjoyed loving relationships and experienced a profound happiness. Ellen chose to demand proof instead of having faith, so she continued to protect herself and remained afraid, angry, and miserable.

Many people argue that they can't tell the truth about themselves *until* they feel loved and safe. But telling the truth about ourselves is required *before* we can feel loved (p. 82). Faith precedes the miracle of love. We can choose to have faith that telling the truth will bring us Real Love and happiness, **or** we can choose to lie and thereby be certain that we'll stay unloved and unhappy. It's that simple.

Every time we interact with people, we make a choice whether we'll exercise faith. When someone attacks you — or when you think they might — I suggest taking the following steps in your mind:

1. "When I attack someone — which includes all the forms of anger — I'm simply afraid and protecting myself. My primary interest is not to hurt them."

2. "Other people attack me with the same motivation."

3. "In this moment, I choose to see that the person attacking me is simply feeling unloved and afraid. They're protecting themselves or trying to get me to make them feel better."

4. "If I react by protecting myself from this person, I can't feel loved, loving, or happy, *and* they will become more afraid and more likely to protect themselves."

5. "I choose to have faith that being truthful and accepting will be more effective than protecting myself."

Taking these steps is far easier when we already feel unconditionally accepted by one or more people. And we need to remember that it is not productive to tell the truth about ourselves to every person we know (pp. 107-8). Some people are not prepared to hear what we have to say.

The Risk of Having Faith

Initially, the thought of exercising faith instead of protecting ourselves is scary. But the actual risk is small. Lying and protecting ourselves can *only* produce the same old feelings of temporary safety and being alone. The chance of finding genuine happiness is zero. On the other hand, even though telling the truth isn't always immediately rewarding, the chances it creates of finding Real Love and happiness are *always* greater than zero. How can we lose? And the reward for our faith is huge: we can finally feel loved and learn to love others, the greatest experience in the world.

We worry that if we trust someone who is actually lying to us or attacking us, we'll be hurt. That fear becomes foolish when we remember that the worst condition of all is feeling unloved and alone. By protecting ourselves, we *guarantee* that we'll feel unloved and alone, exactly what we're trying to avoid. It's ironic that protecting ourselves *causes* the very thing we're protecting ourselves from.

The truth is our only way out. Telling the truth about ourselves (Chapter 10) may be scary in the beginning, but it's far less frightening than the prospect of staying unloved and unhappy all our lives. In short, we have nothing to lose when we exercise faith and tell the truth.

Building Faith

The four steps to finding love (desire, faith, truth, giving up the Getting and Protecting Behaviors) are all connected. Each contributes to the others. As our desire to change grows, telling the truth becomes easier. As we tell the truth and abandon our Getting and Protecting Behaviors (Chapter 11), we feel more loved and our faith grows. As we exercise faith, our ability to tell the truth grows. And so on.

A wise man can help us find faith. As he offers his acceptance and love, we learn that the world is not uniformly critical and conditionally loving. The Wart King learned that from the Wise Man. Wise men and women give us a seed of faith, enabling us to believe that change is possible, that we can be loved and loving instead of afraid, angry, and manipulating. "A wise man introduces the possibility that truth can lead to love, and love to happiness. Faith is choosing to act on that possibility." (*The Wise Man, Telling the Truth and Finding Love*)

Chapter Summary

Without faith, we require proof for each step we take in life. That approach guarantees our continued fear and unhappiness.

When we have faith in the truth and in Real Love, we simply tell the truth about ourselves without manipulating other people or protecting ourselves. It creates the possibility of being truly seen, accepted and loved.

When we choose to have faith in our partners, we trust that they're doing their best as they learn to tell the truth and love us. With that approach, we create far more loving and happy relationships.

Chapter 10

Telling the Truth About Ourselves

Truth → Seen → Accepted → Loved

We cannot feel genuinely loved until we tell the truth about ourselves. Only then can we believe that people see and accept us for who we really are.

Telling the Truth About Ourselves, Not Other People

We enjoy telling other people the truth about *them*, especially about their mistakes and flaws. It makes us feel wise and even superior. But that does not create opportunities for people to see and accept *us*.

Carol complained angrily about her husband to her wise friend, who had heard it all before.

Carol: James is always . . ."

Wise woman: (interrupting) "I've never seen you feel happier after complaining about James. Have *you*?"

Carol was surprised and confused. "Are you taking his side?"

Wise woman: (laughing) "Not at all. He probably does all the things you say and more, but be honest — has it ever made you or James genuinely happier when you complain about him?"

Carol: "But he . . ."

Wise woman: "You can talk about him all you want, but I care about
              you enough to say that talking about *him* won't help you."

Carol: "So what do I talk about?"

Wise woman: "Talk about yourself."

Carol: "Okay. **I** feel angry when James doesn't listen to me or care
         about me."

Wise woman: (laughing) "You're talking about *him* again."

Carol: "No, I'm not. I'm talking about how **I** feel. **I** feel angry. That's
         about me."

Wise woman: "Yes, partly, but you're still criticizing *his* behavior. Try
              speaking without referring to James doing anything wrong."

Carol was speechless, and that's common. Most of us cannot
talk about being unhappy without blaming our partners. We've seen
that pattern from other people all our lives, as in the expression, "You
make me so mad." In the first place, other people *don't* make us
angry (pp. 6-7, 14). In addition, as long as we blame our feelings on
other people, how can *we* ever change the way we feel?

With obvious compassion, the wise woman helped Carol see the
real cause of her unhappiness: Carol had never been unconditionally
loved, a condition that existed long before she met James. When she
married him, Carol demanded that he make her happy, which he
couldn't possibly do because *he* hadn't been loved, either. When James
failed to meet her expectations, Carol felt even more empty and afraid.
Without any intent to cause harm, she then used all the Getting and
Protecting Behaviors with him. She harshly criticized him (attacking)

when he didn't give her what she wanted. She whined and complained that he neglected her (victim). She never admitted that anything was her fault (lying). And when they had a conversation she couldn't control, she often stomped off into the next room (running).

Because Carol felt accepted and loved by her wise friend, she was able to admit her Getting and Protecting Behaviors and see how they affected her marriage. She understood that it was the lack of Real Love in her life and *her* own behavior that caused her unhappiness, not anything her husband did or did not do.

Wise woman: "Congratulations. You just told a lot of truth about yourself, and if you keep doing that, your life will change completely."

Carol: "I've been blaming everything on James for years, but now I see that I've been just as awful to him as I thought he was being to me."

Wise woman: "Yes, you have—and without feeling loved, you couldn't have done any better, so there's no reason to feel guilty. Just see the truth about yourself and allow people to accept you with your flaws. As you feel loved, you'll make much better choices than you have in the past. How do you feel right now?"

Carol: "Amazed. I've never talked about my mistakes like this, and it feels very good. You haven't criticized me or looked down on me at all. I like it."

The Reward for Telling the Truth

Carol's entire life began to gradually change after that single conversation. Without exaggeration, Real Love has that effect. She had never before told the truth about her mistakes in that way and been completely accepted by another person. The feeling that follows that experience is indescribable. The Wart King felt it. I have seen it hundreds of times. And it's available to all of us. As we take the bags off our heads and allow people to see who we really are, we create the opportunity for them to accept and love us. And then we can finally feel unconditionally loved, the feeling we want most in all the world. It starts with such a simple act: telling the truth.

Tell The Truth About What?

We feel accepted and loved only as we tell the truth about the specifics of our lives, not vague generalities. We need to talk about how we feel and how we are behaving. It also helps to understand *why* we are feeling and behaving as we are.

How do we feel?

All our lives, we were trained by the people around us to hide our feelings, especially our fear and anger. When we quarreled as children, we were told, "Stop that right now!" We were taught that being angry was "bad." And we were taught by peers and others that being afraid was a weakness. So when we were afraid or angry, most of us learned to hide it. We learned to lie, which resulted in our feeling unloved and alone.

It's important that we be truthful about the times we're afraid and angry. We need to admit that when we interact with people and wonder if they will like us, we're afraid. The impatience we experience when people inconvenience us is a form of anger. When we become offended by the words or behavior of others, we're both afraid and angry.

If we have not been sufficiently loved unconditionally, feeling afraid and angry is *unavoidable*. Most of us have those feelings many times every day. When we deny them — even unconsciously — we can't feel seen, accepted, and loved.

How are we behaving?

When we feel unloved, empty, and afraid, we naturally react with Getting and Protecting Behaviors. We hide our mistakes (lying), get angry (attacking), act like victims, withdraw from difficult interactions (run), and cling to every morsel of Imitation Love we can find. Until we can be honest about those behaviors, we cannot feel accepted with them — and we certainly can't change them.

Why are we feeling and behaving as we are?

We use Getting and Protecting Behaviors only because we don't feel unconditionally loved and are reacting to our emptiness and fear. It's always that simple. When we do feel unconditionally loved, we don't feel empty, afraid, and unhappy, and we don't use Getting and Protecting Behaviors.

Telling the Truth About Our Mistakes

Being accepted when we're "good" means nothing. When people only like us for being beautiful, successful, and for doing what they like, they don't really love **us**. They like how we make **them** feel. We only feel loved unconditionally when we feel accepted by people who see our mistakes and flaws. It's therefore important that we tell the truth about our imperfections, a lesson the Wart King learned.

When we freely admit our mistakes and see that we're still accepted, we learn that we can be loved while we're wrong, weak, and foolish. When we feel loved under those conditions, what is there to hide? What is there to fear? That's the effect of Real Love.

The Risk of Telling the Truth

It's understandable that telling the truth about ourselves is frightening to most of us in the beginning. But the alternative is to lie about who we are, which guarantees that we'll feel unloved and alone, the worst feelings of all. We really have nothing to lose by taking the bags off our heads.

Where Do We Tell the Truth About Ourselves?
— Wise Men and Women —

We need to be seen, accepted, and loved *while* we're feeling empty and afraid, and on the occasions that we're angry, wrong, and stupid. That's Real Love, and it's the only kind of love that counts. We need to be seen by people who feel loved enough that they're not blinded by their own needs and fears and can therefore see us clearly and accept us unconditionally. We need people who can stay by our side and help us tell the truth even when we protect ourselves by lying and attacking. We need wise men and women.

Where do we find them?

Fortunately, we can all find these men and women who will change our lives. We don't need to go to the top of a mountain, as the Wart King did. We don't need to attend expensive seminars run by impressive institutes and special motivational speakers. We rarely need professional therapy. Wise men and women are all around us, and to find them we only need to tell the truth about ourselves. Wise men are irresistibly attracted to the truth. *Tell the truth and they will come.*

What do we actually say? It's not complicated, but it is different from what we're used to. We talk to people all the time, but we tend to talk about nothing. We talk about the weather, cars, events, and money. We sometimes talk about our feelings, but usually only to complain. For example, we might say that we're angry, but then we blame that on someone else, which helps no one. We need to learn to talk about the things that will change our lives.

I suggest that you make a commitment to try something different in the near future with a friend that you trust. Take a chance and allow that friend to see who you really are, as Carol did on pp. 95-7. The reward can be astonishing. Following are a few examples of some things you could say:

"I was really irritated with my husband yesterday when he didn't do something I wanted (name the specific thing), and then I realized that my anger wasn't his fault. He's not obligated to do everything I want. In fact, I don't have a right to expect him to do anything. But I've been doing that our whole marriage. I haven't been accepting him and loving him at all. Instead I've been making demands and expecting him to change. I've been more interested in my own happiness. I have a lot to learn about relationships."

"My son has had a terrible attitude about a lot of things for some time: school, his chores around the house, the family. And I've really been leaning on him to change all that — restricting him, getting mad at him, stuff like that. Now I'm embarrassed to see that his attitude is *my* fault. All he ever wanted was for me to love him no matter what, and I haven't done that. When he screws up, I get irritated at him, and then he can see that I *don't* love him unconditionally. I didn't understand until now how much that has hurt him. I thought I was a much better father than I really have been."

"My wife did something last night that I didn't like, and I got angry, as usual. But I've been thinking about that lately. We've been growing farther apart for years, and I always blamed it on her. I don't think she's the problem. I haven't been a very loving husband. I've been selfish and critical — much more concerned about what I wanted than what would make her happy. I've never admitted that before, and I feel nervous talking about it now."

"For all these years, I've been working to accumulate all the *things* I could: money, house, cars, job, the usual. But I'm starting to think I've missed something. I haven't paid as much attention to people as I should have."

If you say something like that to a friend and they look at you like you're crazy, you haven't lost a thing, have you? Simply change the subject to the weather or whatever's comfortable, and you will still have the same relationship you had with them before you said anything.

But don't stop there. Keep trying that same conversation with other friends, and eventually, you *will* find someone who doesn't give you a blank, confused stare. You *will* find someone — likely several people — who will say something like, "Wow! That was honest." You will find someone who is attracted to the truth and who will accept you as you are. And they will share the truth about themselves. That's how you find a wise man. They're everywhere, and most of them don't even know who they are. When you finally get that warm feeling of unconditional acceptance from one person, you won't care one bit how many puzzled expressions you got before that. Real Love is worth everything we invest to find it. Everything.

The more we tell the truth about ourselves, the more wise men and women we find. Another useful tool for finding wise men is this book. If you find someone who responds to the truth, you might suggest that they read *The Truth About Relationships*. It stimulates the kind of discussion that will help you develop relationships with people who are genuinely interested in telling and hearing the truth.

The Intermittent Wise Man

It is virtually impossible to find someone who can accept and love us all the time. Fortunately, we don't need that. Feeling accepted for even moments has a miraculous effect, and as those moments become longer and more frequent, the effect grows.

More About the Effect of a Wise Man

After 15 years of marriage, Charlotte and Darrell were "getting along" fairly well. They had come to believe, as most couples do, that the relative absence of major conflict meant that they were happy. But they still sensed that something was missing in their lives. Charlotte talked about that with a wise friend.

Charlotte: "I'm not satisfied with our marriage. But what can I do about it?"

Wise woman: "Right now? Nothing. You can't do anything about your *relationship* until you do something about the one person in the relationship that you are responsible for: *you.*"

Charlotte: "I don't understand. What's wrong with me?"

Wise woman: "If you're unhappy, there's always something wrong with you, and it's always the same thing. You don't feel loved. From the time you were a child, people liked you better when you did what they wanted. That's natural, but it's *conditional* love. What you really needed — and what you need now — is Real Love, which is *unconditional*. But you didn't get that, and *that's* why you're unhappy. Unconditional love is the only thing in life that can make us genuinely happy."

"And then you got married, hoping that Darrell would make you happy, which is understandable. But Darrell had never been unconditionally loved, either, so he couldn't give you what you really needed. You both found yourselves in the impossible situation of starving to death and hopelessly demanding to be fed by each other. *That* is why you feel like your relationship is missing something."

They talked until Charlotte understood how their marriage had become the way it was. There was nobody to blame. Their problem started long before they even met each other. Charlotte also admitted her Getting and Protecting Behaviors and recognized how those had caused much of the conflict that occasionally occurred in their marriage. Charlotte's friend was very understanding and gave examples of doing all the same things herself.

Charlotte: "So it's obvious that Darrell and I need unconditional love. Where do we get it?"

Wise woman: "At this point, neither of you can get the Real Love you need from each other — you simply don't have it to give — so you'll have to get it from people who have it. And *you* can only get it for yourself, not for Darrell. You can do that by consistently telling the truth about yourself to people who can unconditionally accept and love you. As you feel loved, you'll feel that happiness you've been missing all your life. You can talk to me, if you'd like, and I'll introduce you to several other people who are capable of listening to you and accepting you. When you feel loved enough, your life will begin to change."

Charlotte: "But I thought married people were supposed to love each other and not go to other people for that."

Wise woman: "It would be wonderful if all couples could find the love they need *within* their relationship. But very few people have received enough Real Love to be able to share any with their partner. Most partners in relationships simply *can't* love each other, no matter how much they want to."

"Tonight I've learned a lot about you. You're not as happy as you've always pretended to be. You've admitted that you get angry to protect yourself, and that you do other things to manipulate Darrell. Your marriage is not the success you hoped it would be. And you're not capable of unconditionally loving your husband. But even after sharing all those "flaws" about yourself, how do you feel now?"

Charlotte: "Relieved — and surprised. You've been very gentle and accepting toward me. I feel closer to you than ever."

Wise woman: "If you'll keep telling the truth about yourself like this, with people who can accept you, that feeling of being loved will grow and will change your whole life."

Even though Charlotte felt wonderful during the conversation with her friend, in the following days, she forgot the acceptance she'd felt while telling the truth. She became afraid to talk openly about herself again. That's common with people who are just learning to tell the truth about themselves. It takes more than a little love to eliminate the emptiness and fear of a lifetime.

Charlotte chose to handle her relationship with Darrell by herself. But that meant that she unavoidably brought to her well-meaning efforts the same emptiness and fears that she'd always had. She tried to create something new with the same tools. Without the ability to love each other unconditionally, their relationship predictably stayed the same.

After several months of frustration, Charlotte remembered how good she'd felt being loved by her friend, and she made contact with her again, as well as with other wise men and women. She learned to tell the truth about herself regularly and was thrilled at the effect of being seen, accepted and loved. Even though she was not yet able to love Darrell unconditionally, she was much happier herself, and Darrell saw that. The change in her motivated him to start associating with wise men himself, and there he found the unconditional acceptance *he'd* always wanted.

As they each continued to tell the truth, they both felt increasingly loved, safe, and happy. The growth of their relationship was slow at first, but it was real and lasting. Naturally and effortlessly, their relationship became more loving.

We must get loved ourselves before we can love anyone else, and the process of feeling loved begins with telling the truth about ourselves to people capable of accepting and loving us. For more about the powerful role of a wise man, see *The Wise Man, Telling the Truth and Finding Love*. Most of us are capable of becoming wise men.

The Simplicity of the Truth

We believe that our lives are complicated. As we struggle with the many problems we have with our spouses, children, and jobs, it can seen overwhelming. But it only *seems* complicated because we're blinded by our emptiness and fear. As we begin to tell the simplest truths about ourselves, we find the Real Love which eliminates fear and anger, and then we can see everything quite clearly. The truth makes things simple. It's lies that make everything confusing and difficult.

Faith in Telling the Truth

Planting and watering a grain of wheat is an act of faith. We don't know if it will grow, or when. We can only plant it and wait. Similarly, when we tell the truth about ourselves, we plant the seeds of who we are in the hearts and minds of other people. That also requires faith because we don't know which seeds will grow, or when.

The seeds we plant in people who are empty and afraid cannot grow. But that doesn't hurt us. Unloving people can't *take* love from us; they simply can't *give* it. It doesn't matter how many seeds *don't* grow, only that some *do*. The only wise course for us to take is to exercise faith and plant all the seeds we can — to tell the truth about ourselves wherever possible. If we do that, we *will* eventually plant seeds in people who are capable of accepting and loving us as we really are. And, as I said before, we actually *attract* loving people to us.

Groups

Feeling seen and loved by just one person can change our lives completely. When we associate with more than one wise man or woman, we multiply the likelihood of feeling loved. Thousands of people across the country are meeting in small groups with the conscious intent of telling the truth about themselves and loving each other. It is not therapy; there is no financial cost; and there is no formal membership in an organization. These are just "regular people," and the results are life-changing. See the book, *The Wise Man, Telling the Truth and Finding Love* for much more about organizing and telling the truth in groups.

When to Not Tell the Truth About Ourselves

A wonderful sense of freedom comes from telling the truth about ourselves. Even when our partners fail to accept us, telling the truth allows *us* to shrug off the enormous burden of lies that keeps us alone and unhappy. However, it's still not wise to tell the truth about ourselves to everyone:

1. When we express our fear and anger, for example, many people feel responsible in some way. They feel an obligation to help us, which is overwhelming to them if they feel unloved themselves and have nothing to offer us.

2. Telling the truth about ourselves to some people is unnecessarily harmful **to them**. For example, when we understand that our emptiness and fear started in childhood, we may be tempted to share that insight with our parents. But most parents feel threatened by a discussion of their mistakes. To insist that they participate in such a conversation is unloving on our part.

3. In some situations, telling the truth about ourselves is unnecessarily harmful **to us**. For example, if our employer and co-workers knew

everything about our fears and flaws, our careers could be affected in an *unnecessarily* negative way. We do need to be truthful, but with people who are capable of loving us — not with everyone.

How to Tell the Truth
— THE RULES OF SEEING —

Many of us have lied for so long that we really don't know how to be truthful about ourselves. Being honest can be strange and uncomfortable, like learning a foreign language. The following rules or guidelines make it easier for us to see each other. The Rules of Seeing are described further in *The Wise Man*.

I will refer to anyone who is speaking or communicating nonverbally (smiling, crying, withdrawing, sulking) as the *speaker*. The speaker is heard and seen by the *listener* (one or more).

The First Rule of Seeing:
"One speaker"

During any truly productive interaction, there is only one speaker. When two or more people compete to speak, no one is completely heard or seen. I'll illustrate this rule in the next section.

The Second Rule of Seeing:
"Whoever speaks first is the speaker."

Whoever speaks first is the speaker, while everyone else listens. That doesn't prevent anyone from speaking. It only determines the order of speaking and contributes to everyone being heard.

Sarah: "You're always yelling at me and the kids, and I hate it."

Kevin: "I wouldn't have to yell if the house wasn't such a filthy mess."

We all know where the conversation went from there. They exchanged accusations and added even more wounds to their damaged relationship. That always happens when two people try to be heard at the same time. Kevin and Sarah were talking about two separate subjects, and neither was listening to the other. Let's try this interaction again with the help of a wise man and the First and Second Rules of Seeing.

Sarah: "You're always yelling at me and the kids, and I hate it."

Kevin: "I wouldn't have to yell if the house wasn't such a filthy mess."

Wise man: "Sarah spoke first, so let's try letting her finish before we talk about another subject, like the messy house. It really does work better that way, and those are the first two Rules of Seeing that we talked about."

Kevin: "But she . . ."

Wise man: "Think about it. You've already proven with years of experience that when both of you talk at the same time, everybody loses. Do you want to keep doing something that never works, or would you be willing to try something different? If you want to do things this new way, you can still talk about Sarah all you want, but not right now. "

Kevin: "Okay, I'll wait 'til she's done before I talk."

Wise man: "If you plan on talking about her as soon as she finishes, you'll be thinking about what you're going to say instead of really listening to her. And she won't feel like you listened to her, either. I suggest you talk about the dirty house tomorrow or even later."

Kevin had always defended himself when he felt threatened. That made him feel safer for a moment, but the consequences were consistently terrible for both of them: Sarah felt ignored and unloved, and Kevin felt more alone.

After he understood that he would get the chance to speak later — and because he trusted his wise friend — he chose to listen, which created a new and delightful experience for both of them. Sarah expressed herself completely without being interrupted or attacked. She felt seen and understood by Kevin. And he learned things about her that he'd never known. None of that could have happened if they'd both insisted on talking at the same time.

The Third Rule of Seeing:
"The speaker describes himself."

Almost every time someone speaks, he's saying something important about **himself**.

When Sarah said Kevin yelled at her, it would have been a useless distraction to talk about *Kevin* — why he yelled, how often he yelled, or what he said. The real message Sarah was trying to communicate was that **she** felt unloved, frightened, and alone.

While Sarah talked, the wise man listened intently and occasionally helped her express her feelings of fear and loneliness instead of getting lost in the details of past conflicts with Kevin. Even though many of her initial words involved Kevin, the discussion was really about *her*, not him.

As Sarah felt the acceptance and love of the wise man, her anger evaporated. Kevin had never seen her calm down so quickly. Getting angry at her had certainly never done that. In addition, he found that he cared more about her happiness.

The pain of emptiness and fear is overwhelming. In that condition, our thoughts and actions are all centered around protecting ourselves and filling our needs. A wise man knows that, and as he accepts and loves the speaker, that person finally gets what he needs — Real Love. That eliminates the emptiness and fear that are always the real problem in any relationship.

The Fourth Rule of Seeing:
"If you can't be a wise man, get one."

When we're empty and afraid, we're blind to our feelings and to our Getting and Protecting Behaviors. That makes a productive conversation with any partner nearly impossible. A wise man helps us see what we're really feeling and doing. As he accepts and loves us, we can often feel safe enough to stop protecting ourselves. We can then tell the truth about ourselves and see our partners clearly. When we feel nervous, afraid, irritated, or impatient as we're talking to someone, we need to stop repeating our ineffective feelings and behaviors and reach out to feel the love of a wise man or woman.

In the department where Janet worked, a new supervisor took over and began making changes that required more work and flexibility from Janet. She felt threatened by the changes and reacted by marching into his office and having an angry conversation with him. At the end of the day, she called a wise friend.

Janet: "This guy is horrible. He doesn't know anything, but he's already changing my hours and my job description. I'm mad about it."

Wise woman: "You're afraid."

Janet: "What are you talking about?"

Wise woman: "Every time we're angry, we're afraid of something and protecting ourselves. You're afraid of him, and you're using anger to protect yourself."

The wise woman helped Janet see that when the new supervisor ordered things to be done differently, she felt like her opinion didn't matter — which she interpreted as another confirmation that nobody cared about her. She was also afraid that with new job responsibilities, she would make mistakes and be criticized. In short, she was afraid that the new supervisor was creating a situation where he and her co-workers wouldn't respect or like her. Our fears are almost always about not feeling loved.

Wise woman: "You get angry because then you feel less powerless. In addition, when you act irritated and intimidating, you know he might not ask you to do some things you don't want to do. Being angry might get you what you want for a moment, but you'll never be happy that way. You've already proven that a million times over."

Janet: "That's true. So what do I do when I feel angry with this man? It doesn't help to tell him I'm mad, so should I just keep it to myself and pretend I'm not angry?"

Wise woman: "Lying about your anger won't help. You do need to be truthful about that, *but not with him*. When you're angry, share that with someone who can love you while you feel that way."

The next time Janet was angry at work, she stopped talking and said, "I'll be right back. I have to make a phone call." She went into another room and called her wise friend.

Janet: "I'm mad at him again. I want to slap him — he's so stupid."

Wise woman: "What are you afraid of?"

Janet immediately smiled as she realized again that the true cause of her anger was not her boss. She was just afraid of being criticized and not loved. When she saw that, and when she felt loved by her friend, the fear disappeared, along with the anger.

It really is that simple. People all over the country are learning to reach out, tell the truth about themselves, and get loved instead of wallowing in their fear and anger, and they're experiencing dramatic changes in their happiness. Being loved is the most powerful force on the planet.

Chapter Summary

We can feel seen, accepted, and loved only when we tell the truth about ourselves, especially the truth about our flaws and fears.

It's most effective to tell the truth to someone who is capable of seeing and loving us — a wise man or woman. Once we've gotten enough Real Love, our relationships with other people will change.

The four Rules of Seeing make it easier for people to tell the truth and be seen:
  1. One speaker
  2. Whoever speaks first is the speaker.
  3. The speaker describes himself.
  4. If you can't be a wise man, get one.

Chapter 11

Giving Up
The Getting and Protecting Behaviors

Every moment of our lives, we make choices. And then we experience the consequences, which we do not get to choose. When we choose wisely, we're happy; when we don't, we're not. It's really that simple. The consequences of choosing Getting and Protecting Behaviors are always Imitation Love, emptiness, and fear — never Real Love or genuine happiness.

The Deadly Distraction of
The Getting and Protecting Behaviors

Years ago, a man came to my office complaining of a headache. A radiologic scan of his head revealed a large brain tumor.

Me: "How long has your head been hurting?"

Patient: "I'm not sure. Maybe a few months."

Me: "Why did you wait so long before you came to see me?"

Patient: "I don't know. I guess it didn't hurt that much."

Me: "Have you been taking anything for the pain?"

Patient: "I've had some whiskey now and then."

More questions revealed that for several months, this man had been drinking increasing quantities of alcohol to eliminate his pain. Finally, when more than a quart of whiskey per day failed to give him adequate relief, he came to see me. By that time, however, the tumor had become too large to treat.

This man died because he treated his *pain* instead of treating the *cause* of the pain. Similarly, when we use Getting and Protecting Behaviors — and the Imitation Love that those behaviors gain for us — we treat our pain instead of addressing the real problem, which is the lack of unconditional love in our lives. The result is deadly, as in the case of my patient.

Giving Up the Getting and Protecting Behaviors
— More Faith —

Real Love is freely offered *and* received (pp. 45-7). When we manipulate people, we can't freely *receive* anything, even if it's freely *given*. Until we stop manipulating people with Getting and Protecting Behaviors, we can never know what it's like to feel Real Love.

Although Getting and Protecting Behaviors are dangerous, few of us are eager to give them up because we've used them since childhood to get the only kind of "happiness" we've ever known. Imitation Love feels good temporarily, and in the absence of Real Love, we're understandably reluctant to give up our enjoyment of praise, power, and pleasure.

Elaine had never been loved unconditionally. Empty and afraid, she constantly manipulated people and protected herself. She acted like a victim, lied about her mistakes, and exaggerated her accomplishments. She attacked the people who dared to criticize her, and she clung tightly to those who gave her any attention. Predictably, with all those Getting and Protecting Behaviors, she never found Real Love, and her relationships were frustrating and unsatisfying.

A friend suggested that Elaine contact a group of wise men and women. Elaine did that, but instead of talking about her own mistakes and selfishness, she talked about how badly her husband and others treated her. She was given many opportunities to tell the truth about herself, but she chose to manipulate people for praise and sympathy instead. Because of that, she was unable to feel the Real Love she was offered, and she remained empty and frustrated. Eventually, she left the group, as miserable and alone as the day she arrived.

Like Elaine, Susan was also empty, afraid, and unhappy. She associated with the same group of wise men and women Elaine had known. But unlike Elaine, Susan decided to exercise faith in the ability of people to love her as she told the truth about herself — without manipulating them. They helped her identify the times she lied, attacked people, and acted like a victim — and she listened. That made it possible for her to *feel* the Real Love she was offered, the same love that Elaine could not feel because of her refusal to tell the truth about herself. Feeling a love and happiness she had never known, Susan no longer had a reason to use her Getting and Protecting Behaviors, and was increasingly able to give them up.

Many people say: "I don't think I can tell the truth about myself. It's just too hard." On the contrary. Telling the truth is far easier than the complicated and never-ending effort of lying, getting angry, acting like victims, and otherwise protecting ourselves and getting Imitation Love. Telling the truth about ourselves doesn't require more effort, just more faith (Chapter 9).

The "In-Between Time"

Most of us are quite inexperienced with exercising faith and telling the truth about ourselves. For that reason, we don't usually feel unconditionally loved the first few times we attempt to give up the Getting and Protecting Behaviors we've used all our lives. Between the time we give up Imitation Love and the time we feel Real Love — the "in-between time" — we may feel as though we have no source of happiness at all, which is frightening to us. When we feel afraid and don't yet feel loved, we tend to reach out for the familiar and predictable pleasure of Imitation Love.

Faith

When we believe the world to be unloving and harsh, we naturally see evidence everywhere to support our belief. We even see attacks where there are none. But when we simply *choose* to have faith in the possibility of being loved, we see the evidence of people accepting and loving us much faster, and the "in-between" time becomes much shorter.

Telling the Truth and Feeling Loved

We have a lifetime of old feelings and behaviors to overcome. The more often we tell the truth to people capable of seeing and loving us, the sooner we feel seen, accepted, and loved. We can make the "in-between time" very brief indeed.

Chapter Summary

We use Getting and Protecting Behaviors to decrease our pain. But those behaviors also make us feel unloved and alone, the worst pain of all.

Until we give up manipulating people with Protecting and Getting Behaviors, we can never know what it's like to feel Real Love.

Chapter 12

Gratitude

There are few things that contribute more to happiness and loving relationships than gratitude. Without it, we miss all the joy of feeling loved and loving others.

Ingratitude

Jack and Patricia had an unsatisfying relationship filled with the exchange of Imitation Love. On the occasions when they got what they wanted from each other, they were relatively "happy." But when their expectations were not met, their disappointment and anger clearly revealed the emptiness of their relationship.

They talked to a wise friend who taught them about Real Love and the process of finding it. Jack started telling the truth about himself to some loving men who accepted him unconditionally. He began to feel genuinely happy for the first time in his life. Patricia was skeptical and chose to do nothing. After several weeks, they met again with their friend.

Wise man: "Have either of you noticed any difference in your relationship?"

Patricia: "No. Jack still watches television all the time and ignores
me."

Wise man: "Jack, in the past twenty-four hours, have you spent any
time with Patricia?"

Jack: "This afternoon, I sat in the kitchen and listened to her talk about what she did all day. I called her from work during my lunch break, just to see how she was doing. And we talked for half an hour in bed last night."

Wise man: "Patricia, do you remember those things?"

Patricia: "Well, yes, but he still sits there in front of the television and . . ."

It's true that Jack still watched a lot of television, but he was learning new things and was beginning to change his feelings and behavior toward Patricia. We don't become loving overnight. We learn to be loving in the same way we learn anything else — we practice, and the progress is gradual. When we're not grateful for the small steps people take, we don't see their progress, which guarantees that we'll continue to be disappointed and unhappy with them, as Patricia was with Jack.

Expectations

Being ungrateful is a natural result of having expectations. When we suffer the pain of emptiness and fear, we feel justified in expecting other people to drop what they're doing and help us. Those expectations destroy happiness (pp. 60-1). When I expect you to give me five apples and you only give me three, I can't possibly be grateful for the three I get. I effectively ruin the enjoyment of your gift by focusing on the two apples I *don't* get. What a pity. When we don't get what we expect, we're always disappointed. Even when we do get what we expect, the best we can feel is not disappointed, which is a lot less fun than feeling loved and grateful.

Gratitude

Being grateful is a decision we make, and it creates joy in every experience.

Gary and Melissa had a relationship filled with Imitation Love, much like Patricia and Jack. Neither intentionally used or hurt the other, but they both used Getting and Protecting Behaviors that made Real Love impossible between them.

They talked to a wise friend, who taught them about Real Love and the process of finding it. Gary started telling the truth about himself to some loving men who accepted him unconditionally. He began to feel genuinely happy for the first time in his life. Patricia was too afraid to do the same, but she did choose to believe that Jack was trying to do something different, and she watched him with interest. After several weeks, they met again with their friend.

Wise man: "Have either of you noticed any change in your relationship?"

Melissa: "Something is different about Gary. This afternoon, he sat in the kitchen and listened to me talk about what I did all day. It was great. Earlier, he called from work just to see how I was doing. And we talked for half an hour in bed last night, something we hadn't done in a long time. This is better than Christmas."

Wise man: "In the past, you complained that he watched television all the time. Does he still do that?"

Melissa: "Sure, he still watches TV a lot, but so what? He also spends time with *me*, and it's obvious that he cares about me. I'm loving every minute of this."

Gary: (to Melissa) "I'm enjoying our time together, too — more than I thought I would. And I love seeing you happier."

Gary didn't do any more for Melissa than Jack did for Patricia, but the result was vastly different for Melissa because she chose to be grateful for her experiences with Gary instead of complaining about what she didn't get.

Gratitude is not a trick of positive thinking. Gratitude is a choice we make to simply acknowledge the truth about what we have, which greatly amplifies our enjoyment of everything we receive.

Patricia's failure to appreciate her husband's efforts was not malicious. She was just empty and afraid to exercise faith that change was possible. But her choice to be skeptical nonetheless destroyed any possibility of enjoying a loving experience with Jack. In addition, her ingratitude was discouraging to him, making it harder for him to continue his efforts to love her.

We need to be grateful for our own growth as well as the progress of others. We can't become perfectly loving in a day. We learn with practice. When we don't recognize the positive steps we take, we become discouraged and stop trying.

Grateful FOR, not TO

From childhood, we were taught to be grateful **to** the people who do things for us. If we failed to express our gratitude when people gave us an ice cream cone or birthday gift, our mothers usually said, "Now what do you say?" In effect, we were forced to say "Thank you" to the people who gave us anything.

We like people to be grateful **to** us. When they do that, we appear to be gracious and generous. We use the gratitude of others to make us feel good. That's Imitation Love.

In contrast, it's quite healthy to be grateful **for** what we have. Gratitude magnifies the enjoyment of every experience and opportunity. With it, we feel energized, hopeful, and happy. When we're grateful, envy and disappointment disappear, and we feel closer to the people who love us and to those we love.

Chapter Summary

When we choose to be grateful for the love we receive, we see it more clearly and feel it more powerfully. Ingratitude only leads to disappointment and unhappiness.

Chapter 13

The Effect of Real Love

As we feel unconditionally loved, we lose our emptiness and fear, and then we no longer have a need for Getting and Protecting Behaviors. When we stop lying, being angry, attacking people, acting like victims, and running, our relationships can only become more loving and rewarding. Real Love changes everything.

Mark and his wife had always traded Imitation Love with each other: approval, praise, time, attention, and sex. In the beginning, they were relatively content with that. It was exciting, and it was the only kind of "happiness" they'd ever known. But after a year of marriage, as the thrill of Imitation Love evaporated, they both became increasingly dissatisfied with their relationship. Mark talked to a wise friend who described the process of finding Real Love and genuine happiness.

Mark: "I don't understand how talking about my mistakes will make me happy."

Wise man: "You don't need to *understand* it. You need to *experience* it, and that takes faith. You can only feel loved and happy *after* you actually tell the truth about yourself, and that requires faith on your part. What have you got to lose? How can it hurt to try something different? Do you like the way your life is going now?"

Mark: (laughing) "No."

Mark began to tell the truth about himself, to his friend and to a few other loving men and women. They helped him see how often he lied, attacked people, acted like a victim, and ran from relationships. Mark felt accepted by these people as he took the bag off his head and allowed them to see who he really was, warts and all. One day Mark phoned his friend.

Mark: "I just had an amazing conversation with my wife."

Wise man: "What happened?"

Mark: "She was furious at me for something I promised to do and then forgot about. When she does that, I usually get angry, too, and then everything goes into the toilet. But this time, I was feeling great because of the conversations I've been having with you and the other people I've been talking to. So when she got angry at me, I didn't get upset."

Wise man: "It makes quite a difference to feel happy, doesn't it?"

Mark: "Big difference. Because I felt loved by you and the others, there was nothing to be upset about. This is great."

Wise man: "What did you say to her?"

Mark: "I put my arms around her and told her I'd been thoughtless and selfish, not only then but on many occasions. You wouldn't believe what she did then: she cried. It was incredible. I wish I'd done this a long time ago."

Wise man: "You couldn't have. You didn't feel loved enough to do that before now."

Mark and his wife gradually developed a delightful relationship.

That is the effect of Real Love. When we exercise faith and tell the truth about ourselves, we begin to feel the love that banishes emptiness and fear. We can then choose to climb out of the bottomless pit of Getting and Protecting Behaviors.

Imagine that you're down to your last two dollars, and you're hungry. Putting the money on a table, you get ready to go out and buy some bread. Suddenly, I dash into the room, snatch the two dollars off the table, and run away before you can stop me. Almost certainly you would be angry at me.

Now imagine that I do exactly the same thing — steal the two dollars — but this time you have twenty *million* dollars on the table, and it's all yours. How would you feel this time? You wouldn't even care. The loss of two dollars is nothing when you have twenty million.

That's how it feels to have Real Love. It's like having twenty million dollars all the time. When we feel unconditionally loved, everything else becomes insignificant. When people fail to do what we want, we see their behavior as the small inconvenience that it really is. Heavy traffic becomes a tiny nuisance, not something that makes us angry and unhappy. When people speak badly of us, we're not threatened; we understand that they're simply afraid and protecting themselves. And so on.

This is not a fairy tale. Many people are experiencing these powerful changes in their feelings and behavior as they practice telling the truth about themselves and enjoy the fulfillment of unconditional love.

The Frequency of Feeling Real Love

Like almost everyone, Stacy had been conditionally loved as a child. As a teenager, she became increasingly rebellious, and by the time I met her — at age nineteen — she had been through several miserable relationships with men and was drinking and using drugs.

Stacy called me at the recommendation of a friend. As we talked about the mess she had already made of her life, she was surprised and delighted at how accepted she felt. I recommended that she tell the truth about herself every day with myself and some women who were capable of loving her. She called me several times in the following weeks, but then she gradually went back to the familiar and reproducible pleasures of Imitation Love. It's very easy in the beginning for the first feelings of real acceptance to be overwhelmed by the effects of a lifetime of emptiness and fear. She made no contact with me for a year.

When she finally called again, she was living with an abusive man and using cocaine every day. We talked in my home.

Stacy: "Life sucks."

Me: "Are you serious about doing something different this time?"

Stacy: "What do you mean?"

Me: "Do you remember what I recommended when we talked the last time?"

Stacy: "Sort of. You said I should talk with some people, but I did that."

Me: "How often did I suggest that you do that?"

Stacy: "Are you saying that I have to do this your way? That doesn't sound like unconditional love to me."

Me: "I care about your happiness no matter what you do. That's what unconditional love is. But I've also learned that changing a lifetime of unhappiness requires more than a casual effort. If you really want to change the direction of your life, you need to tell the truth about yourself and feel loved *consistently*. When you do that, everything will change. If you only do it occasionally, nothing will happen. You don't have to do anything to please me."

Stacy came to my home every day for several weeks. In addition, she called once or twice a day, just for reassurance that she was still loved. One day, she bounced into my office and sat down with a huge grin. She was no longer in an abusive relationship, and she hadn't used any drugs in three weeks.

Stacy: "I'm glad you talked straight to me when I first came to you a few weeks ago. You didn't exactly say I was being lazy, but I was. I wasn't taking this seriously, and I needed to. Now that I've been talking to you every day, I've been feeling more loved and happy than I ever have in my life."

Stacy subsequently learned to develop healthy relationships with many people and is now a very happy person.

When we put our whole heart into finding unconditional love, the result is infinitely rewarding. But when we make half an effort, the result is not half of infinite — it's usually nothing at all. Half-measures are often worthless, like putting half of the wheels on a car.

Real Love is the greatest treasure of all. It's worth whatever effort we expend to find it. It's worth any risk we take. When we tell the truth about ourselves consistently, we create the opportunity for Real Love to completely overpower our emptiness and fear. And then we experience the kind of happiness that becomes our entire reason to live (p. 10).

Chapter Summary

When we feel unconditionally loved, we have the greatest gift of all. Real Love eliminates emptiness and fear, and then we no longer have a need for Getting and Protecting Behaviors.

To experience the healing effect of Real Love, we need to tell the truth about ourselves consistently.

Learning to Love

Chapter 14

Learning to Love
Loved → See → Accept → Love

The joy of being loved is indescribable, but the joy of loving others is even greater. Once we feel loved, learning to love others is easy:

1. First we must feel **loved** ourselves.
2. Feeling loved, we're no longer blinded by emptiness and fear. And then we can **see** other people clearly.
3. When we see people as they really are, **accepting** them is natural and effortless.
4. When we accept people, we unavoidably develop a concern for their happiness. And that is Real **Love**.

We discussed the first step in chapters 7-11. In Chapters 15-17, we'll examine steps 2-4 in the process of learning to love.

Again, We Must Feel Loved First

Michelle and her husband constantly manipulated each other for approval and defended themselves against each other's criticism. She attended a seminar that I taught on the subject of relationships. Dutifully, she wrote down what I said and eagerly went home to try out what she'd learned. She called a few days later.

Michelle: "At your workshop, you gave examples of what couples say to each other as they're learning to be truthful and loving. I used those exact words with my husband, but it didn't work at all. He actually got angry at me. It was awful."

Me: "When your husband didn't respond as you hoped, how did
           you feel?"

Michelle: "I was very disappointed. But I didn't tell him that."

Me: "Sure you did. You communicated your disappointment —
           and your anger — with your choice of words, your facial ex-
           pression, your tone of voice, and the way you moved your
           body. You're doing some of that with me now, and you can
           be certain that he saw and felt all of it. And then he felt at-
           tacked and protected himself with anger."

We think we hide our feelings, but they leak out all over the place,
and Michelle realized that as we discussed it for a minute or two. She
also understood that I wasn't criticizing anything she'd done.

Michelle: "So what do I do now?"

Me: "Do you remember the first step in learning to love other
           people?"

Michelle: "No."

Me: "You have to feel loved yourself before you can love your
           husband and change your relationship."

Michelle: "I do feel loved."

Me: "I know you believe that, but it's simply not possible. If you
           felt unconditionally loved, you would not have felt disappointed
           and angry when he didn't do what you wanted."

We then talked about what she could do to find Real Love for
herself. We must understand the importance of *feeling* loved before
we can *give* it. We can't give what we don't have.

Chapter 15

Seeing

We see people clearly when we see them as they really are — with all their needs, fears, flaws, and strengths — instead of seeing what we want from them or fear from them. And we must see people clearly before we can love them unconditionally.

When we don't feel loved ourselves — when we're empty and afraid — we can't see people clearly. Without Real Love, we can only see what people might do *to* us or *for* us. We can't see who they really are. We're blind, and that condition inevitably leads to expectations, disappointment, intolerance, and feeling alone.

Expectations and Intolerance

While we're experiencing the intolerable pain of feeling unloved, we feel justified in expecting other people to give us whatever we want. Blind to anyone's needs but our own, we cannot tolerate anyone who will not help us. But most of the people around us don't feel unconditionally loved, either, so they naturally focus entirely on filling *their* needs. Incapable of giving us the happiness we expect, they even do things that inconvenience and hurt us. Our disappointment in others — and conflict with them — is therefore guaranteed.

Alone

When we can't see other people clearly, they effectively disappear. When we see them only as objects that either serve or hurt us, who they really are does not exist for us. Obviously, we are then alone, the condition we fear the most.

Learning to See

We can learn to see people clearly. But it's not a technique we learn from a book. Our failure to see is a natural result of the blinding effects of emptiness and fear. *Seeing clearly is therefore the natural result of eliminating emptiness and fear with Real Love.* No other approach to seeing will work.

As we begin to feel unconditionally loved, the Rules of Seeing (pp. 108-13) also help us to see other people. Kevin (pp. 108-10) had never really listened to Sarah. He was so empty and afraid that he only saw what she could do for him or to him. When a wise man helped him apply the First Rule, he saw Sarah more clearly, and their relationship began to change.

Rewards of Seeing Clearly

When we see people without distortion, the world ceases to be a place where we feel threatened and alone.

Beauty

All the "unattractive" behaviors of human beings — attacking, accusing, manipulating, selfishness, anger, etc. — are just reactions to emptiness and fear. But we can only see that when we feel loved and safe ourselves. When we feel loved, we no longer find people "ugly" when they use their Getting and Protecting Behaviors — they're just drowning and trying to survive (pp. 11-15).

Richard was always angry about something, and people tended to avoid him. Because I met him at a time when I felt unloved and unhappy myself, I also judged him harshly and did my best to stay away from him. As I learned to tell the truth about myself, I felt more loved and was less blinded by my emptiness and fear. I saw that Richard was not intentionally offensive, just afraid. He attacked people to protect himself, not primarily to hurt them. He became a different person entirely when I saw him clearly.

The world is a beautiful place when we see it clearly, as are all the people in it. That perspective changes our relationships dramatically.

Not alone

When we see people clearly and interact with who they really are, we feel an immediate connection to them. We're no longer alone, and that's a wonderful feeling.

No More Anger or Hurt Feelings

When we see people clearly, we know that they're only afraid and protecting themselves when they get angry or otherwise attack us. It no longer makes sense to be angry at them or offended by them when they do those things. Without resentment and anger, relationships naturally become more loving.

No More Guilt

Our anger and selfishness are also just reactions to emptiness and fear. It's just as foolish to feel excessively guilty and ashamed about our own mistakes as it is to be angry at others for getting Imitation Love and protecting themselves. Without Real Love, we're doing the only things we know to survive.

As Wayne told the truth about himself, he felt the love of wise men and women who saw and accepted him. Freed from the blinding effects of emptiness and fear, he saw for the first time that he had not been loving toward his children. And then he felt a terrible guilt about it.

Wayne: "I did so many things to hurt my children. How can I ever be forgiven?"

Wise man: "What did you do?"

Wayne: "Whenever they got in my way, I was angry and criticized them. I only thought of myself and failed to give them the love they needed. I hurt them a lot."

Wise man: "Were *you* feeling unconditionally loved at the time?"

Wayne: "Hardly."

Wise man: "You can't give love to anyone when you don't have it yourself. That doesn't change the pain that your children experienced, but you gave them all the love you had. You were empty and alone, so you could not have loved them unconditionally. Feeling guilty about that is a waste of time, energy, and happiness. All you can do now is tell the truth about your mistakes and feel the acceptance of loving people. As you feel loved, you'll be able to share that with your children."

Some guilt is useful. It motivates us to see our mistakes and learn from them. But prolonged guilt is an unnecessary and destructive burden that actually interferes with our ability to see and love the people around us.

Seeing and Change

How we see the world entirely determines what we say and do. As we feel unconditionally loved and learn to see clearly, the whole world changes before our eyes, and loving other people becomes a natural and effortless consequence.

Chapter Summary

When we're blinded by our emptiness and fear, we can't see other people clearly. We only see what they can do for us and to us. We're demanding, intolerant, and alone.

As we get Real Love, our needs and fears diminish, allowing us to see people more clearly and accept them. We're no longer alone, and anger and guilt disappear.

Chapter 16

Accepting

When we see people clearly, accepting them becomes natural and effortless.

Why We Fail to Accept People

There are only two reasons we don't accept people as they are:

1. We *want* something from them and don't get it. When we feel unloved, we cannot accept someone who fails to give us what we want.

2. We're *afraid* of them because they're criticizing us, mocking us, or avoiding us — or because they *might* do those things. How can we possibly accept someone we're afraid of?

In short, we don't accept people because **we** are empty and afraid. The solution to our intolerance is obvious. We need to feel unconditionally loved, which eliminates emptiness and fear.

Ellis had a critical opinion about everyone: black people, poor people, women, fat people, foreigners, politicians, his neighbors, policemen, and so on. But he had one friend who could see that he was just unloved, empty, and afraid, and his wise friend taught Ellis about

Real Love. Ellis learned that his emptiness and fear blinded him to other people, but he found that difficult to believe.

Ellis: "Are you saying that if I felt loved and saw people clearly, I'd love everybody?"

Wise man: "Yes."

Ellis: (laughing) "No way. I could never love a woman who was ugly and fat."

Wise man: "Without feeling unconditionally loved yourself, you can only see people as a source of Imitation Love—praise, power, pleasure, and safety. I'm your friend, and I tell you this because I care about you. When you look at a woman, you're too selfish to see who she really is. You only see how she could make **you** happy—by giving you something beautiful to look at, or flattering you, or being an object for your sexual fantasies."

"If a woman offers you those things, you like her. That's Imitation Love, because your concern is for *your* happiness, not hers. You don't love 'ugly, fat' women because they can't give you the kind of Imitation Love you want."

"I'm not criticizing you in any way, just describing what you're doing. When you get enough Real Love, you'll be able to see who people really are, and then you'll see how beautiful everyone really is. And then you'll accept the people you now think are 'ugly.'"

Without Real Love, we only see people as objects that will or will not give us what we want. When they don't, we reject them and criticize them for being too rich, poor, tall, short, black, white, fat, skinny, beautiful, unattractive, etc. It's the lack of love in *our* lives that causes all the disgust, prejudice, racism, and hatred in the world.

Evidence of Not Accepting

Most of us *say* we accept our partners, but our behavior says otherwise.

Rick and Mary had been married for several years.

Mary: "I'm not happy with our relationship."

Wise man: "In what way would you like it to be different?"

Mary: "I wish he could just accept me and not criticize everything I do."

Rick: "But I do accept you."

Mary: "No, you don't. You're always telling me what's wrong with me: the house isn't clean; my hair isn't the way you like it; I'm too fat; I can't cook . . ."

Wise man: "Rick, do you say those things?"

Rick: "Hardly ever."

Wise man: "Mary?"

Mary: "He doesn't usually say it with words, but it's all over his face and in his tone of voice. And when he's angry, he stays in another room and doesn't touch me."

Wise man: "Rick, are you aware that you do those things?"

Rick: "Not really."

Wise man: "I believe that. Having spoken with you before, I know that you have felt unloved and empty all your life. In that condition, it's understandable that you feel a big disappointment every time Mary doesn't do exactly what you want — like clean the house. Without being aware of it, you communicate that disappointment to her in many ways, and she feels it."

The wise man went on to explain how that disappointment was poisoning their relationship. He also made it clear that Rick's disappointment was not Mary's fault.

We generally don't accept people as they are. We say we do. We wish we did. We know we should. But we don't, and we prove that with our disappointment, anger, criticizing, withdrawing, and controlling.

Disappointment

Without Real Love, we're miserable, and then we naturally expect our partners to help us feel better by giving us what we want. When they don't, we're disappointed. We tend to believe that other people exist for the primary purpose of making us happy, and when they don't, we judge their behavior to be unacceptable.

Disappointment is so common among people that we believe it's a normal and unavoidable reaction when we don't get what we want. We're disappointed that other drivers aren't more courteous, that our boss isn't more appreciative, that our spouse isn't more cooperative and loving, that our children aren't more grateful, and so on. We need to understand that disappointment is absolute proof that we don't accept people and things the way they are. Disappointment is selfish and wrong.

Rachel and Vicki had been friends for years, but Vicki was becoming increasingly irritated with Rachel.

Vicki: "Whenever we talk on the phone, it's only because I make the call. Rachel never calls me."

She said this to a wise woman who understood that when we're unhappy, **we** are not feeling loved and are therefore incapable of loving our partner.

Wise woman: "The problem here is that you don't accept Rachel as she is."

Vicki: "But I do accept her. I just don't like it that she never calls me."

Wise woman: "How do you feel when Rachel doesn't call you?"

Vicki: "I'm disappointed and hurt. How could I not be?"

Wise woman: "When you're disappointed, Rachel correctly hears that she has failed to meet your expectations and is therefore not acceptable to you. That's the only thing disappointment can mean, and she feels it. Your concern is for *your* happiness, not hers."

Because Vicki trusted that her wise friend cared about her, she listened and realized that she did want Rachel to change. As she told the truth about her selfishness, she felt accepted by this wise woman. Feeling loved *with* her flaws gave Vicki a sense of peace and happiness that enabled her to see and accept Rachel.

For many years, my sighs and frowns of disappointment communicated this message to my children: "I accept you only when you do what I want. When you don't, I love you less." That's what disappointment means. Most of us heard that message from our parents, and we have passed it on to our spouses, children, friends, co-workers, and others. We don't intend to do it, but we declare with our disappointment that our partners have failed to please us and are therefore defective and unacceptable.

When children sense that we don't accept them, they believe that something is wrong with them. As adults, we all carry the scars of many interactions where our parents and others were disappointed in us. That's why we learned to protect ourselves with lies, anger, acting like victims, and running. That's why we learned to seek the pleasures of Imitation Love with Getting and Protecting Behaviors.

Anger

Anger is a tiny step past disappointment, and is always selfish and unloving. As long as we feel that way, we cannot have loving relationships with anyone.

Controlling

When we attempt to control the behavior of other people, we deny their right to make their own choices and learn in their own way. That is not unconditional acceptance, and it ruins the possibility of loving relationships.

The Illusion of Acceptance

Early in a relationship, the flow of Imitation Love is often generous and satisfying. "Falling in love" is an obvious example. When we're trading Imitation Love, we often believe we're accepting our partner when the truth is we're just getting everything we want from them. It's easy to confuse satisfaction with genuine acceptance. The conditional nature of our acceptance is revealed when we feel disappointed on the occasions we don't get what we want.

Learning to Accept Others

We learn to accept others as we feel unconditionally loved ourselves and understand the Law of Choice (p. 55).

Feeling Loved

Our own emptiness and fear are the entire reason we don't accept people. In that condition, we can't accept those who hurt us or don't give us what we want. When we feel unconditionally loved, emptiness and fear melt away. Accepting people then becomes natural and effortless.

Understanding the Law of Choice

We all have a sacred, inviolable right to choose for ourselves what we think, say, and do. That is the Law of Choice. Without that right, we're nothing but tools in the hands of those who make our choices for us. When we understand that, we also accept the right of every man and woman to make their own mistakes, even those that inconvenience and hurt *us*. How could we not? Imagine a world where we could determine the choices of other people. We'd all become nothing more than a stage full of puppets fighting to control each other. There could be no loving relationships.

Accepting Other People —
How It Looks

Most of us have never seen a relationship where the partners genuinely accept each other. It's a beautiful thing to behold.

Peace

Trying to change other people is a lot of work. Expectations, disappointment, blaming, and anger are exhausting. We eliminate all that when we accept people as they are. What remains is a deeply satisfying peace.

Effortless

Real acceptance flows naturally from feeling loved ourselves. It's not something we work at. When we're "trying" to accept someone, we're almost certainly failing.

I'm Sorry and I Forgive You

When people make mistakes that inconvenience us, almost all of us expect them to apologize, and then we generously consider whether we will bless them with our forgiveness. But if I truly accept you, why would I ever require you to apologize to me for making the mistakes that are unavoidable in the process of learning? You really do have the right to make your own choices, including the ones that inconvenience *me*. Demanding apologies is selfish and arrogant, and forgiveness is unnecessary when we truly accept people.

One evening I realized that my ball-point pen was missing. I asked my children if anyone had seen it.

Benjamin: "I borrowed it. I took it to school, and now I can't find it. I'm sorry."

The true meaning of "I'm sorry" is usually "I'm sorry I got caught." Or "I hope you'll be less angry at me if I say I'm sorry." We mostly apologize to look good and to get out of trouble. It's far more useful to simply see that we made a mistake and learn how to choose differently than it is to apologize.

Benjamin had participated in many family discussions about telling the truth and being responsible, so I said, "Being sorry doesn't mean much. Tell me instead what your mistake was."

Benjamin: "I was selfish. I needed the pen, so I took it from your desk without thinking about you at all. When I lost it, I didn't want to get in trouble, so I didn't tell you about it. I hid my mistake, and that's lying."

Me: "Excellent. You know what you did wrong, and now you're less likely to make those choices again. I'm happy for you. How do you feel now?"

Benjamin: "Relieved. I always feel better when I tell the truth and you still love me."

When we truly accept our partners, we understand that they must make mistakes in the process of learning. We don't insist that they apologize. We have faith that when they see their mistakes, they're less likely to repeat them. I am not saying there is no place for a sincere and selfless apology, but in our family, we rarely apologize. We simply see our mistakes, admit them, and learn from them.

Acceptance Does Not Mean Approval of Bad Behavior

It's possible to condemn unloving and destructive behavior while still accepting the person exhibiting that behavior. However, *most people do not do that*, despite their vigorous claims to the contrary. It's quite common for people — especially parents — to say, "I love you, but I'm angry at your behavior." *That is a lie* we use to justify our anger. When we genuinely accept someone, we never feel disappointment or anger as we describe their mistakes. While people feel unconditionally loved, they don't get angry.

Benjamin lost my pen because he made a selfish choice, and he needed to see that. But if I had been angry at him, I would *not* have been loving *him* and condemning *his behavior*. I have corrected my children with anger on many occasions, and it is always wrong. I have tried to justify my behavior by saying that I was only angry at their behavior, not them, and it was always a lie. Anger is never justifiable. It is always selfish.

In addition, being angry at Benjamin would not have helped him in any way. He only needed to know that he'd made a mistake — which on this occasion he knew without me telling him — and that I accepted and loved him *while* he was irresponsible and inconvenient. If he had not understood his mistake, it would have been my responsibility to point it out, but without disappointment and anger. He learned an important lesson the same way I've learned most of my lessons — by making mistakes. I accepted that — and him. People learn far better while feeling loved than they do while feeling our anger.

Consequences

Accepting someone does not mean we can't impose consequences for their poor choices. For example, if a child carelessly wrecks the family car — which has happened in our family — he may benefit from paying the increase in insurance premiums that result from the accident, or not driving for a specified time. A discussion of the imposition of consequences with children can be found in *The Truth About Parenting*.

In an ideal society — where everyone was unconditionally loving — imposing consequences would be entirely unnecessary. When people made mistakes, they would see them, admit them, and try to not make them again. But we don't live in such a place. People often don't learn from their mistakes. Many people lie about their mistakes and insist on repeating them, even when they injure the people around them. And that is why consequences must sometimes be imposed, to *require* people to live with some negative effect of their behavior and thereby motivate them to not repeat that behavior. Sometimes the offender can't be motivated and must simply be restrained so that the rights of others are protected. Employees who repeatedly perform below a declared standard must eventually be disciplined in some way. Citizens who consistently violate the rights of others and ignore all attempts to teach them must eventually be physically restrained.

However, we must be careful how we impose consequences. If we apply them with anger, they become punishments, which rarely benefit anyone. Punishment only heightens the fear and anger of the person being punished, which makes him even more likely to use Getting and Protecting Behaviors in the future. He is then *more* likely — not less — to require future punishment, and then we haven't helped anyone.

When we punish others in anger, we also hurt ourselves. Anything which interferes with our ability to feel loved and love others is bad (pp. 24-5). Although it is true that even the most loving consequences will not change the behavior of some angry people, we who administer the consequences still benefit greatly as we apply them in a loving way. Being loving is always happier than every other way of living.

Accepting and Leaving

Accepting someone does not mean we have an obligation to spend time with them. When I feel loved, I can easily accept someone who uses dangerous drugs and is violent, for example, knowing that he is simply choosing Getting and Protecting Behaviors because he feels unloved and afraid. But I have no obligation to spend my free time with him. More about leaving relationships in Chapter 27.

Chapter Summary

We only fail to accept people when we're empty and afraid. When we feel unconditionally loved, accepting other people is natural and effortless.

Everyone has a right to learn by making their own choices and mistakes. When we don't accept people, we're saying that other people don't have the right to choose when it affects *us*.

When we're disappointed, angry, critical, and controlling, we are not accepting people. And then we're alone.

We learn to accept people as we find Real Love for ourselves, and as we understand the principle of choice. Accepting others gives us great peace and eliminates the need for apologies and forgiveness.

We can accept people unconditionally without being obligated to accept their behavior.

Chapter 17

Loving

As we feel loved, the blinding effects of emptiness and fear disappear. We can then see people clearly and accept them, after which we naturally and effortlessly begin to care about their happiness. The entire purpose of relationships is to provide opportunities for us to practice loving each other and to experience the profound joy that always follows.

Learning to Love —
And Forgetting That We're Loved

We *learn* to love just like we learn anything else. It takes time and practice, and in the beginning, we don't do it very well. The most important ingredient in that process is feeling loved ourselves. When we feel unconditionally loved, it's natural and easy for us to accept and love the people around us, and that is exciting — for us and for them.

But remember this: when we're first experiencing unconditional love, those few moments of acceptance from wise men and women are opposed by a lifetime of *not* feeling loved. Sometimes — because love is a powerful force — those loving moments succeed, and then we feel loved and capable of loving others. But when the environment becomes too stressful — when we're with people who are too demanding and critical — we often forget about those who love us. We just *forget*. And then we become afraid and go back to the old and familiar Getting and Protecting Behaviors without thinking. In that condition, we're unable to love anyone.

As we continue to tell the truth about ourselves and feel more loved, our confidence grows and we forget less easily. With more experience receiving and giving Real Love, we become capable of loving other people better and more consistently.

We don't need to feel guilty for the mistakes that we unavoidably make as we learn to be loving, even when those mistakes cause pain for our children, spouses, and others. Too much guilt actually becomes an obstacle (pp. 137-8). We can't freely tell the truth about ourselves and feel loved while we feel ashamed. Instead of feeling discouraged or guilty, we simply need to be truthful about the times we're unable to be loving. And then we can find someone to love us, which is the only way to become more loving.

Sandra had been learning how to tell the truth about herself for several months. She had experienced some wonderful moments of unconditional love, and she was beginning to see and accept her husband Charles.

One afternoon Charles came home in a bad mood and was unpleasant to Sandra. In the past, Sandra would have been angry about that, or she would have avoided him entirely. However, because she was feeling loved, Sandra remained happy and didn't feel threatened by Charles's behavior. She then tried to help him feel better, but he resisted everything she did and actually became more irritated. Eventually, it was more than Sandra could handle. She said something hateful and stomped out of the room. She called her friend on the phone and told her what happened.

Sandra: "I don't think I'll ever get this. Just when I thought I'd learned something about being loving, I blew up again. I'm disgusted with myself and discouraged."

Wise woman: "I've made many mistakes like that, and I'll make many more. So will you. You don't need to feel guilty about it. Just see the truth about what you did and know that you're loved while you're making your mistakes."

Sandra: "I guess I'm feeling too stupid to feel loved."

Wise woman: "As you started talking to Charles this evening, you did feel loved, and because of that, you were able to reach out to him and try to help him. You cared about his happiness, and that's Real Love. But you've only recently begun to feel loved yourself, and when Charles kept being angry, you felt threatened and briefly forgot that you were loved. It was simply too much for you at this stage in your growth, so you went back to protecting yourself with anger. That's natural."

"Now you're feeling guilty about mistakes that you *have to make* as you're learning how to love people. I've heard you play the piano, and you do it beautifully. But when you were a child, didn't you made lots of mistakes while you were practicing? And was it stupid of you to make those mistakes?"

Sandra: "No. Mistakes are just part of learning how to play."

Wise woman: "It's the same with learning to love people. You don't feel loved enough yet to love other people consistently. Instead of feeling frustrated about it, just recognize that you made an unavoidable mistake. As you feel more loved, the things people do won't empty you out as easily as they do now. Eventually, you'll be able to keep loving Charles even when he's angry and difficult."

One-Sided Loving

In the beginning, we all need to be loved by people who are willing to stay with us while we learn to tell the truth and feel their love. We need to be loved while we have nothing to give in return, and while we still use Getting and Protecting Behaviors. *Our partners need the same experience.* Are we willing to sometimes be the one to do that for them? Are we willing to love a partner who gives us little or nothing in return? If not, we'll never learn to be loving and will not have loving relationships.

Sandra took the step of telling the truth about herself and experiencing unconditional love with some wise men and women before Charles would even think of doing such a thing. For quite some time, therefore, it was unavoidable that she had more love to give than Charles had. There was nothing "unfair" about that. In virtually every relationship, one partner is farther along in the process of feeling loved and loving others than the other partner is. Sandra was willing to continue loving Charles despite the many times he had nothing to give her. That willingness is indispensable to the growth of a relationship.

Many people refuse to give love in a relationship when they're not immediately rewarded with something in return. They abandon their relationships whenever the exchange of love is "unfair." Such people cannot create loving relationships. Before a relationship can break out of a pattern of self-protection and trading Imitation Love, one partner must be willing to tell the truth about himself and find unconditional love *without any promise of cooperation from the other*. He can then bring that love back to the relationship, which will then unavoidably change. Waiting on our partner to take the first step, or even to cooperate and take each step after us, is selfish and unproductive.

Charlotte (pp. 102-5) would never have seen an improvement in her relationship with Darrell if she had insisted that he take each step that she took. She wisely decided to do whatever it took to find Real Love for herself first, and *after* she did that, Darrell was motivated to do the same for himself.

Loving is Effortless and Natural

Once we feel sufficiently loved, it's natural that we care about the happiness of others. Giving Real Love is effortless, while trading Imitation Love is hard work — it requires lying, attacking people, acting like victims, and otherwise manipulating people. When loving other people feels stressful, that's a sure sign that we're not loving them unconditionally. We're somehow trying to get something for ourselves: praise, power, pleasure, and safety. Manipulating people and protecting ourselves is exhausting. Real Love is not.

We Can All Be Wise Men and Women

As we feel loved and learn to see and accept other people, we obviously become wise men and women for those who need to be seen and loved. Sometimes we're able to do that for only moments at a time, but those moments are very important for us and for the people who are drowning (pp. 11-15). The more loved we feel, the longer and more frequently we are able to function as wise men.

Chapter Summary

As we get loved ourselves, and as we practice seeing and accepting others, we gradually and naturally learn to become more loving.

In most relationships, one partner must be willing to be more loving than the other.

As we learn to be loving, we will make many mistakes. But in the process, we can all learn to be wise men and women.

Loving

Chapter 18

Mutually Loving Relationships

A mutually loving relationship — where both partners selflessly care about the happiness of the other — is the most delightful experience in the world. We all **want** that, but few of us are prepared to **be** the kind of truly loving partner that such a relationship requires. Before we can participate in a mutually loving relationship, we must learn to tell the truth about ourselves, feel unconditionally loved, and learn to love others. We can't play a duet until we first learn how to play an instrument by ourselves.

Telling the Truth About Ourselves

When we know that our partner loves us no matter what mistakes we make or how we inconvenience them, why would we ever need to lie or otherwise protect ourselves from them?

Henry: "Did you make the bank deposit?"

Elizabeth: "No, but I'll do it tomorrow."

Henry: (obviously irritated) "You said you'd do it today."

Elizabeth paused: "You're right. I did say that, but then I chose to do some other things that I thought were more important. I was selfish and made a mistake."

Henry's anger visibly decreased.

For most of their relationship, when Henry got angry, Elizabeth became afraid and protected herself. She claimed that her mistakes were not her fault (lying). She acted hurt and offended (victim). Sometimes she expressed her anger at Henry (attacking) for not appreciating her. And occasionally, she just walked off in tears (running, victim). Those Protecting Behaviors made her feel safer for a moment, but they also made her feel even more distant from Henry.

However, at the time of their interaction above, each of them had been telling the truth and feeling loved by wise men and women — and by each other — for more than a year. Because Elizabeth felt loved, she didn't become afraid when Henry attacked her with his anger. Without the distractions of emptiness and fear, she saw Henry clearly and knew that his anger only meant that he was temporarily empty and afraid. She then had no need to protect herself and was able to tell the truth about her own behavior instead.

Telling The Truth About Our Partner

Elizabeth could see that Henry was still unhappy because he was angry, and she knew that he would feel better if he could tell the truth about that and feel her acceptance of him.

Although the general rule is that it's best to tell the truth about *ourselves*, occasionally we can help our partner by telling them the truth about *them*. When they feel empty and unloved, telling the truth about themselves is exactly what they need in order to feel seen and accepted. But when they're empty and afraid, they're unable to be truthful without help. They're too busy defending themselves. So they need someone to help them see the truth about their feelings and behavior. But that does *not* give us the automatic right to speak. Two important conditions need to be met before we should consider telling someone the truth about them:

1. We need to be unconditionally loving. If we can't provide the un-

conditional acceptance that someone needs while they hear the truth about themselves, we need to be quiet. If we tell the truth about them without Real Love, they will feel attacked, which leads to more fear and Protecting Behaviors. If we feel disappointed, angry, or afraid, we need to keep our opinions about other people to ourselves.

2. The person we're talking to needs to be capable of hearing what we're saying. Even if we feel loving, there are many times that other people are too afraid to hear what we have to say. If we push them too hard, they can only respond with Getting and Protecting Behaviors rather than feel accepted and loved. And then we haven't helped them at all.

In a mutually loving relationship — where there have been many unconditionally loving experiences in the past — our partner may feel safe enough that we can help them tell the truth about themselves. That creates the opportunity for them to feel even more accepted and loved. That was Elizabeth's goal. Before she spoke, however, she honestly examined her feelings to be certain that she felt no anger or need to be right.

Elizabeth: "You seem angry."

Henry smiled as he sensed that Elizabeth was concerned about him, not accusing him of anything or trying to stop him from being angry.

Henry: "All day I work with people who don't understand me or care about me. When you didn't make the bank deposit, I thought you didn't care about me, either, and I protected myself by selfishly lashing out at you. Sometimes I forget that you love me."

Elizabeth: "That's understandable. When I chose to do other things instead of the bank deposit, I *was* selfish and didn't care about you as much as myself. And for years, I made that kind of decision all the time."

They held each other and enjoyed the happiness that only comes from being honest, feeling loved, and loving someone else.

Henry: "It helped me a lot that you didn't defend yourself when I got angry. Thanks."

A potential confrontation was transformed into a loving experience. These miraculous interactions are common in mutually loving relationships — and we can all learn to have them.

Telling the Truth All the Time

Elizabeth bought a new dress and put it on before going out to dinner with Henry.

Elizabeth: "Do you like my dress?"

Most of us feel trapped by questions like that. We're afraid of offending our partner and then being the object of their disappointment or anger. In a mutually loving relationship, the answer is easy.

Henry: (hugging Elizabeth) "I love you no matter what you wear."

From someone who loves their partner, that is not a way of avoiding a potentially difficult question. When we feel loved and unconditionally love our partner, everything else — clothes, money, physical appearance, etc. — take their proper place in life. They become insignificant.

On this occasion, however, Elizabeth really wanted an opinion about the dress. Although she felt loved by Henry, she still worried a little about what other people thought of her physical appearance.

Elizabeth: "I'm glad you love me, but I still want to know what you think of the dress. Would I look better in this or something else?"

Henry: "That's not my favorite dress. You look more attractive and sophisticated in the other clothes you wear."

Because they had a mutually loving relationship, Elizabeth knew that Henry's comment was about the *dress*, not *her*. She appreciated his opinion, and it helped her make the decision to take the dress back.

When two people know they're loved by each other, they have what they've always wanted most. Anything else isn't worth getting anxious or offended about.

One evening, Elizabeth came into the room where Henry was watching a basketball game. Elizabeth didn't enjoy watching sports and was looking forward to watching a movie after a long day at work.

In the past, when Henry and Elizabeth did not have a mutually loving relationship, Elizabeth felt trapped and angry when Henry watched something on television that she didn't enjoy. She judged that Henry didn't care about her, and most of the time, he didn't. She then criticized him angrily (attack) for not caring about her. Or she whined about how he never considered what she wanted (victim). Or she left the room and sulked for hours (running). Every little thing — watching television, spending money, disagreements about the children, etc. — became a huge source of contention between them. Without Real Love, every crumb of Imitation Love becomes very important, and we feel compelled to grab it and protect it.

On this occasion, however, Elizabeth felt loved and happy. She and Henry had been practicing telling the truth and loving each other for some time.

Elizabeth: "How much longer will the game last?"

Most of the time, when people ask questions like that, it's an indirect attack. What they really mean to say is this: "I can't believe you're watching television again. And of course you're watching something I hate. How much longer are you going to sit there keeping me from watching what I want?" But Elizabeth had no such hidden meaning in her question. She was simply gathering information that could influence her next question or decision. That's what real questions are for.

Henry: "They haven't been playing long, so it will probably go for another two hours or so."

Elizabeth: "I was interested in watching a movie, but if the basketball game is important to you, I'll do something else."

Henry: "I am enjoying the game, but it's not a big deal. I wouldn't mind watching a movie."

With minimal effort, they chose a movie they both enjoyed.

Henry did not "give in." If the basketball game had been sufficiently important to him, he would have said so and Elizabeth would have done something else. Because Henry felt loved, he knew he did not have to change what he was doing to make Elizabeth happy. And if he had chosen to watch the game, she would not have been angry because she knew that Henry loved her. People don't feel angry when they know they're loved.

In every relationship, there will always be conflicts between specific interests, preferences, and schedules. But when two people care about each other's happiness, those conflicts are easily resolved, as Elizabeth and Henry demonstrated. And again, disappointment and anger are never involved while people are loving each other. More about conflict in Chapter 25.

Faith in Mutual Love

Nathan and Dena had practiced telling the truth and loving each other for years. On Dena's birthday, her friend Julie called.

Julie: "What did Nathan give you for your birthday?"

Dena: "Nothing."

Julie: "How disappointing! Did he forget about it?"

Dena: (laughing) "No, he didn't forget. Nathan is my best friend in the world. Every day he tells me he loves me — with his words and the things he does. He smiles and touches me every time he sees me. He accepts and loves me no matter what I do. How could I want more than that for my birthday?"

Dena and Nathan had developed a relationship with enough love that Nathan didn't have to constantly prove his love to Dena, even on her birthday. Because Dena chose to remember and trust their many loving experiences together, she saw the evidence of his love everywhere, instead of seeing every little mistake or omission as a sign that he didn't care about her. She had faith that Nathan was doing his best to love her, even on the occasions when Nathan paid her little attention or actually became irritated with her. With that attitude, she felt loved all the time.

It's unfortunate that most people give birthday and Christmas gifts — at least in part — because they feel they have to prove their affection to their partners. And they're afraid of the consequences of not giving a gift. That sense of obligation is not compatible with Real Love.

One

In a mutually loving relationship, the partners become one. They're united in their desire to contribute to each other's happiness. There is no score-keeping. Both partners fill the needs of the other because they want to. They don't do it so their partner will be grateful, nor do they serve each other to avoid their partner's displeasure.

Exclusive Relationships

An exclusive relationship is one where the partners agree to make each other the primary focus of their attention. Marriage is an example (Chapter 19). An exclusive relationship is not required for happiness. This contradicts what we've been taught from an early age, that in order to be really happy, we must "go steady," have a lover, get married, etc. — if we don't, something must be wrong with us.

A mutually loving relationship naturally develops between any two people who feel unconditionally loved. It does not have to be exclusive. We can have that kind of relationship with many people, not just one. Divorced, widowed, and single people with several mutually loving relationships are far happier than married couples or lovers who have an exclusive relationship without Real Love as its foundation.

Chapter Summary

In a mutually loving relationship, the two partners tell the truth about each other, have faith in each other's love, and enjoy profound happiness. They become one.

Loving and being loved by the same person is the greatest experience in life. We can learn to have that experience with many people, not just an exclusive partner.

Chapter 19

Marriage

Half the marriages in this country end in divorce, and most partners who stay married are not experiencing the joy of an unconditionally loving relationship. They just avoid major conflict and call that "happiness." Clearly, most of us are confused about what marriage is and how it works.

The Expectations of
Falling in Love and Getting Married

Without unconditional love, we desperately gather every scrap of praise, power, pleasure, and safety we can get. When we find someone who gives us those things consistently, or when we think they might, we develop a powerful hope that they will continue to do that and make us happy. When our anticipation of getting Imitation Love from a specific person is great enough, we call that feeling "falling in love." We fall in love with someone because they make *us* feel good. That is not Real Love.

After falling in love, we naturally want to guarantee a consistent supply of that feeling. And *that* is almost always why we get married, to ensure that someone will be there every day to make us happy.

We're not entirely selfish. We do have *some* concern for the happiness of our spouse. But without feeling unconditionally loved ourselves, we can only be empty and afraid, and in that condition, our *primary* motivation for getting married is selfish. When we're starving to death ourselves, it's very difficult to be primarily concerned about the needs of anyone else. Many of us deny the selfishness in our marriages, but we prove it every time we're disappointed when our partner fails to give us what we want.

The Marriage Vows

When two people get married, they exchange promises which all boil down to this: "I will always love you more than I love anyone else." That's what each partner *says*, but they both *hear* their partner say much more:

> "I promise to make you happy — always. I will heal your past wounds and satisfy your present needs and expectations — even when you don't express them. I will lift you up when you're discouraged. I will accept and love you no matter what mistakes you make. I give to you all that I have or ever will have. And I will never leave you."

Neither partner is consciously aware of making those many promises, but their partner still hears them and insists that they be fulfilled. Without unconditional love, both people have an impossible task, no matter how hard they try. Disappointment and anger are then guaranteed.

The Truth About Expectations

When we feel empty and unloved, we understandably expect the people around us — especially those who claim to love us — to make us feel better and give us what we want. In the case of a spouse, where marriage commitments have been exchanged, we feel especially justified in having our expectations. But expectations are always selfish — even in marriage, the Law of Choice still applies (p. 55).

Bruce complained for several minutes about his wife, Paula.

Wise man: "Obviously, you're angry at her."

Bruce: "Of course I am. Who wouldn't be? All she does is complain. This isn't a marriage anymore. We haven't even had sex for months."

Wise man: "I haven't had sex with Paula for all those months, either, but I'm not angry."

Bruce: "That's different! She's my wife!"

Wise man: "So what?"

Bruce: "She's *supposed* to have sex with me. We're married!"

Wise man: "You believe that because you're married to Paula, she's *obligated* to have sex with you — and to do many other things that make you happy. You can't have a loving relationship with Paula as long as you keep expecting her to change who she is for your convenience."

The wise man then talked to Bruce about expectations, the law of choice, Getting and Protecting Behaviors, and unconditional love.

Most of us get married so we can feel justified in demanding that our partner make us happy. When they don't do that, we insist more urgently, which guarantees our disappointment and anger. Marriage is not a whip with which we force our spouse to give us what we want. As long as we use it that way, we'll never be happy.

The Truth About Marriage

So what is marriage? *Marriage is a commitment* we make to stay with our partner while *we* learn to unconditionally love *them*. It's an agreement to stay in a relationship for a lifetime, even when our partner is not loving. It's also a commitment to limit the sharing of some things (living together, sex, financial resources, etc.) to one partner. That may not be a romantic definition of marriage, but it is clear and useful.

Bruce became increasingly unhappy with Paula.

Bruce: "I want a divorce."

Wise man: "Why?"

Bruce: "I'm miserable. Paula just doesn't understand me. She . . ."

Wise man: (interrupting) "Paula is not the cause of your unhappiness. You felt unloved and empty long before you met her. And then you expected her to make you happy, but she couldn't do that because she'd never been unconditionally loved, either. She didn't make you unhappy. She just couldn't meet your expectations to change your whole life."

"When you married Paula, you made a commitment to continue this relationship even when it became difficult. Now you have an important opportunity to learn how to love her — and how to love other people. If you leave her now, you'll learn nothing and will repeat the same mistakes in your next relationship."

Without the commitment of marriage, we tend to leave our relationships when we're uncomfortable. And then we learn nothing.

Alice's husband was totally incapable of loving her. But she learned to tell the truth about herself and felt accepted and loved by several wise friends. For several years, she tried to share that with her husband, but he remained afraid, angry, and alone.

Wise woman: "Why do you stay married to him?"

Alice: "You stayed with me while I learned to tell the truth and feel loved. When I married my husband, I promised to do the same for him."

It's easy to love someone who loves us in return. Alice chose to continue loving someone who didn't love her. By doing that, she learned a great deal about Real Love.

Divorce

When I talk about the lifelong commitment of marriage, I am not saying there's never a reason to dissolve a marriage. More about that in Chapter 27.

Other Committed Relationships

We can have other relationships where the long-term commitment is similar to that of marriage — with parents, children, siblings, and some friends. All these relationships give us powerful opportunities to learn about Real Love.

Chapter Summary

We get married because we hope that our partner will take the responsibility for making us happy. Our expectations make disappointment and unhappiness inevitable.

Marriage does not give us the right to have expectations of our partner. It is simply a commitment to stay with our partner while we learn to love them.

Chapter 20

Sex in Relationships

We are surrounded by references to sex — in books, television programs, movies, magazines, newspapers, radio, billboards, calendars, and in the jokes and stories we tell each other. The depiction of sexual desire and activity—sometimes subtle, but often quite graphic — has become so common that we accept it as normal. Sex is portrayed as a healthy appetite to be gratified as casually as eating a meal. We admire and envy sexually attractive men and women, and we're convinced that if we're sexually appealing ourselves, we'll feel worthwhile and happy.

What We Get From Sex

Sex is a powerful source of Imitation Love.

Praise

In the absence of Real Love, we desperately want to be valued for something. We then settle for earning the praise and admiration of other people. When someone finds us sexually attractive, we feel acceptable, important, and even lovable.

Brenda was fifteen years old. Although her parents did their best, they had no idea how to love her. As a result, she felt worthless and alone. But there was a bright spot in her life. A sixteen-year-old boy at school, Matt, thought Brenda was beautiful, and he communicated that profusely as he looked at her and talked to her. That was more attention than she'd ever received, and for the first time she could remember, she felt worthwhile.

Matt was not primarily concerned for Brenda's happiness. He liked how *he* felt when she looked at him, talked to him, and allowed him to touch her. When Matt's expressions of affection became increasingly sexual, Brenda cooperated without hesitation because Matt made her feel important, and she was willing to do anything to keep that feeling. It's little wonder that she ignored her parents and others who warned her about the dangers of her behavior.

Eventually, when the thrill of using Brenda faded, Matt abandoned her to find entertainment somewhere else. Brenda was briefly devastated, of course, but she also learned from this experience a pattern of behavior that would bring her pleasure all her life. She discovered that if she was sexually appealing, boys and men would praise her and "love" her. That felt a great deal better than being ignored or criticized.

Although we're often not aware of it, sexual attraction is a very important criterion for most of us as we choose a partner. We like to think we're above such a primitive motivation, but our thoughts and actions betray us. When we fantasize about the perfect partner, do we picture a man or woman who is physically unappealing? No, we don't. Physical appearance matters a great deal to us. Which of us seeks out a stimulating conversation with the least physically attractive man or woman at a social gathering? Without thinking about it, we treat physically "ugly" people differently than those who are obviously beautiful. Put a gorgeous model and a fat, "unattractive" woman in any group of men and see if the two women are treated the same. Unthinkable.

This emphasis on physical attraction is everywhere. When a friend introduces their child to us for the first time, we feel a pressure to say something about their appearance, don't we? Even in the bedtime stories we tell our children, the princess is always beautiful and the prince is handsome. At an early age, our children learn that beautiful people consistently get more attention and "love" than those without that characteristic. So our children work to be physically attractive, and if they don't succeed, they believe they're defective. Why else would anorexia and bulimia be epidemic among young women? Physical appearance affects virtually every relationship we have.

Many of us deny that we have this fixation on sexual attraction: "There's nothing wrong with enjoying physical beauty. It's like admiring a great work of art, or piece of literature, or an exceptional skill." Ridiculous. Do we prefer one nose or pair of lips over another because it conforms to some *mathematical* model? Do we admire long, wavy hair because it's more *functional* than a balding scalp? Do we enjoy large breasts because they're *artistically* more pleasing than a flat chest? No. We need to be honest and admit that most of us are attracted — however unconsciously — to physical characteristics that are *sexually* appealing. Models are not chosen for magazine covers and billboards because of their intellectual characteristics — and we can't get enough of them.

Power

The greatest power of all is the ability to choose how *we* feel and behave. We have that power when we feel loved. With Real Love, we have genuine happiness, and then, no matter what other people do, we can choose to feel loved, loving, and happy. We can choose our reaction to any situation.

But when we don't feel loved, we're powerless. In response to our emptiness and fear, we can only choose Getting and Protecting Behaviors. In the absence of Real Love, power is the ability to influence — a socially acceptable word for "control" — the behavior of other people, and sex offers a great deal of that. Although Brenda was powerless with her parents and most others, she discovered that with sex she could persuade boys to do almost anything. If we can't have what we want most — Real Love — the power to control other people is intoxicating.

Pleasure

The physical pleasures of sex — sight, sound, touch, taste, and smell — are intense. When our lives are otherwise unfulfilling, sex provides an immediate thrill so powerful that we're often willing to risk serious social, emotional, health, and even criminal consequences to get it.

The Irrelevance of Physical Appearance in Relationships with Real Love

If we unconditionally care about the happiness of another person, why would our love be affected *in any way* by the physical appearance of that person? Why would we care more about the happiness of a beautiful woman — or man — than an "ugly" one? We wouldn't. But we do not love our partners unconditionally, as proven by the fact that we really are more attracted to physically beautiful and sexually attractive people.

The Danger of Sex

In the ancient Greek epic, Odysseus struggled mightily to return home to his family, and in the process, he was required to overcome great trials placed in his path by jealous and angry gods. At one point in the journey, his ship passed an island where the Sirens lived. Those mysterious bird-women produced a song so beautiful that sailors were completely enchanted and mindlessly steered their ships toward the captivating sound, where they broke up on the rocks of the island.

Sex is like the song of the Sirens. People without Real Love are powerfully attracted to sex, and as they pursue it, they lose their direction, fatally distracted from their journey toward real happiness. And then they break up on the rocks of Imitation Love, destroyed by emptiness, disappointment, and misery.

Real Love is the only thing that will ever make us genuinely happy. Anything that distracts us from telling the truth and finding Real Love is potentially deadly. *That* is the danger of sex. It *distracts* us from finding unconditional love. In the absence of Real Love, sex is so enjoyable that when we get enough of it, we think we're truly happy. And then we see no reason to tell the truth about ourselves and find Real Love. Few activities have caused more unhappiness than the misuse of sex.

Real Love is based on the truth. If we experience the pleasures of sex with someone early in a relationship — before we know who they really are and before we've shared the truth about ourselves — we become hopelessly confused. We lose our sense of what's true and what's real. We cannot distinguish between genuinely caring about our partner's happiness and simply enjoying how they please us sexually.

In high school, Amy felt unloved and alone, and she envied the "beautiful" girls who seemed to get all the attention and have all the fun. As she got older, Amy became more physically attractive, in part because she worked at it. She enjoyed the attention and praise she received for being sexually appealing. And when men tried to win her approval, she felt powerful.

Amy became obsessed with looking good and attracting men. What she really wanted — without understanding it — was to be unconditionally loved, but she settled for attracting men with her appearance and behavior. They found her sexually exciting, and she found the relationships briefly satisfying, but the excitement always wore off. She then worked even harder at being seductive, but eventually, she discovered — as millions of others have — that no amount of sexual attention could make her happy.

Many of us cannot feel worthwhile unless we're having a sexual relationship. In our society, we actually view people as defective if they don't have a sexual partner. When we can't have a satisfying sexual relationship with a real person, we turn to fantasies fueled by the pictures in magazines, videotapes, the Internet, etc. The unspeakably large pornography industry — which includes many mainstream and socially acceptable motion pictures — proves our addiction to sex as a substitute for Real Love and genuine happiness. Sexual pleasure is advertised everywhere as the ultimate thrill and evidence of success and worth. Tragically, without Real Love, sex is always bad — as defined on pp. 24-5 — and only leads to unhappiness.

Solutions to the Dangers of Sex

The unrestrained gratification of our sexual desires has become widely accepted as normal. But without Real Love, sex causes incalculable emptiness and misery, and we ignore that at great peril. Those who dare to speak of these dangers are commonly labeled as old-fashioned, judgmental, and morally intrusive.

Get Loved

When we tell the truth about ourselves and find Real Love, we lose our sense of emptiness and fear. We no longer have to fill ourselves obsessively with the hollow pleasures of sex and the other forms of Imitation Love.

Only In Marriage

The dangers of sex are drastically reduced when we only share that experience with our spouse. From the beginning of time, societies have prescribed marriage to prevent the enormously destructive effect on stable relationships and families that is caused by indiscriminate sex.

Steven: "I've been dating a woman for two months, and I think I love her. But I'm not sure if it's unconditional love. How can I know?"

Wise man: "Are you having sex with her?"

Steven: "Yes."

Wise man: "Then it's almost impossible for you to know if it's Real Love. While you're enjoying the enormous praise, power, and pleasure of having sex with this woman, it will be very difficult for you to clearly sort out whether you genuinely care about *her* happiness (Real Love), or whether you just like how she makes *you* feel (Imitation Love). Have you had sex with other women?"

Steven: "Sure."

Wise man: "And in the beginning of those relationships, did you think you loved them?"

Steven: (smiling) "Yes, I did, and I think I get the point you're making."

Wise man: "How did those relationships turn out?"

Steven: "Obviously, they didn't, because I don't still associate with any of those women. While I was having sex with them, we had a lot of fun, and I really thought I was in love. But when the sex wore off, we didn't have much of a relationship anymore."

Steven quit having sex with his girlfriend and soon discovered that he didn't really care about her happiness, only his own. He learned that he was still too selfish to unconditionally love anyone. Sobered by that experience, he began the process of telling the truth about himself and finding Real Love.

Teaching Our Children

What we learn in childhood we tend to carry throughout our lives. If we really want to eliminate the unhappiness caused by misuse of sex in the world, we need to teach our children. We need to teach them about Real Love. Even better, we need to love them unconditionally. They need to understand that sex is a natural expression of affection to be shared between two people who have made a lifetime exclusive commitment to each other. They need open discussions about sex that include guidance about dating, relationships, masturbation, pornography, how to have a conversation about feelings, and so on. For all that, I suggestion reading *The Truth About Parenting*.

Sex in Unconditionally Loving Relationships

When two people care about each other's happiness in a committed, exclusive relationship—marriage—physical intimacy is a natural and delightful result. In the presence of Real Love and life-long commitment, sex is great fun.

Bruce and his wife Paula (pp. 170-2) were both unhappy with the sexual part of their marriage. After talking with his wise friend, Bruce realized that he was being selfish and had been concerned only about what she could do for *him*. He learned to tell the truth about himself and began to feel unconditionally loved. He started to care about Paula's happiness instead of using her for his own pleasure.

Paula felt his concern for her, and that changed everything. She felt enormously attracted to him, emotionally and physically. They began to enjoy sex regularly, and it was a more fulfilling experience than anything they'd ever known before. Bruce said to his wise friend: "I don't even know what word to use for what we used to do, because having sex now is a completely different experience than that it used to be."

For ages, men have pressured women to have sex and wondered why they resist. The answer is simple: nobody likes being used. Women want men to care about their happiness, which is impossible if a man is pushing a woman to give him something she doesn't want to give. When men and women have a mutually loving relationship, they almost always have an equal desire to express their affection sexually. There is no aphrodisiac in the world equal to knowing that your partner genuinely cares about your happiness (Real Love).

Sexual Dysfunction

Sex has become an awful experience for many of us. We worry about the adequacy of our sexual performance. We're afraid that our partner doesn't find us sexually desirable. And many of us live in constant anxiety that our partner will touch us sexually, because we can't stand the thought of being used again by this person who doesn't really love us. Emptiness and fear utterly destroy the pleasure of sex. Impotence is often caused by fear. When people feel unconditionally loved, most sexual dysfunction disappears.

Chapter Summary

We use sex to get praise, power, and pleasure, all forms of Imitation Love.

In the absence of Real Love, sex is distracting and dangerous. When we feel unconditionally loved, sharing sex with our partner becomes a delightful and loving experience.

Chapter 21

Friends, Family, The Workplace, and Everyone Else

The only worthwhile goal of any relationship is to receive and/or give Real Love. We can practice telling the truth, feeling loved, and loving other people as we associate with friends, family members, business associates, and even total strangers.

Friends

Relationships without the truth are useless because there's no possibility of sharing Real Love. People who lie are not "bad," just protecting themselves when they're afraid and getting Imitation Love when they feel empty. However, the consequences of lying are still severe. If our friends cannot tell the truth about themselves, they cannot feel the love we give them, nor can they love us. And that means we can't have a worthwhile relationship with them.

If I choose to tell the truth about myself and my friend does not choose to do the same, we are by definition walking in different directions and can't possibly have a real relationship. When I choose to quit associating with that friend, I am not abandoning him. I'm just accepting *his* decision to go in a different direction than myself. It's better to recognize that an honest relationship does not exist than to continue having unrealistic expectations of another person.

I'm not suggesting that we abandon every friendship at the first hint of dishonesty. That would make relationships impossible. More about leaving relationships in Chapter 27.

Choices

Lewis and Ray lived an hour apart, and for years they had been meeting every Wednesday for dinner. Because Ray didn't like to drive, they met near his house most of the time.

Lewis: "It's not fair. We always do whatever's convenient for Ray, and I'm tired of doing all the driving."

Wise man: "A relationship is the natural result of people making independent choices. You can only observe Ray's choice and then make your own."

Lewis: "But I do all the driving, and I think . . ."

Wise man: "You're describing what you *want*. Ray has chosen to drive less than you do, and he gets to make that choice. Now, what do *you* choose to do?"

Lewis: "But it's not fair . . ."

Wise man: "Irrelevant. You can only make *your* choice. So far, you've chosen to do most of the driving. But you've also chosen to resent Ray and try to change him, and *that's* what's making you unhappy, not Ray."

The wise man then explained the other choices available to Lewis (pp. 56-63):

1. Lewis could quit trying to change Ray, but still resent him for the unequal travel involved. His relationship with Ray would then be strained and unhappy (live with it and hate it).

2. Lewis could continue traveling and simply enjoy the time he got to spend with Ray (live with it and like it). This choice would only be possible after Lewis learned to tell the truth about himself and felt unconditionally loved. He could *tolerate* an "unfair" relationship with Ray without feeling more loved himself, but he couldn't *enjoy* it.

3. Ray's choice to not drive did not obligate Lewis to do anything. Lewis could choose to drive less himself by simply meeting with Ray less often. They'd have less time together, but Lewis would be less inconvenienced and resentful (a variation on living with it and liking it).

4. Lewis could choose to end his relationship with Ray (leave it). That would almost certainly be happier than the constant manipulation of trying to change Ray, and the frustration and anger involved with failing.

Lewis's friend also explained what he had learned about Real Love, expectations, and relationships.

We always have a choice. We can try to change people and resent them when they don't do what we want, but that choice guarantees *our own* unhappiness. Or we can allow people to make their own choices, accept them as they are, and enjoy loving relationships with them.

Lewis chose to tell the truth about himself to people who could love him. As he felt loved, he began to see Ray clearly and accept him instead of expecting something from him. He felt more loving toward Ray and decided that he was willing to keep doing most of the driving. He also saw that his selfishness had ruined many other relationships over the years.

When we try to change other people, we choose to be miserable. Most of us prove that every day, but we continue to do it.

Family

Families give us the opportunity to practice loving people in committed relationships, much like marriage does.

Parents and Children

See Chapter 22.

Siblings

I overheard two of my children, Benjamin and Janette, talking in the next room:

Benjamin: "You're wearing my shirt again! And then you never put anything back. Don't touch my stuff!"

Parents often step in at this point and resolve the dispute. When they do that, they create peace for themselves, but they rob their children of valuable opportunities to learn about seeing and loving each other.

I could easily have made this conflict go away *for me* by telling them to stop arguing, or by telling Janette to not touch Benjamin's stuff again. I used that approach for years. But there was a more important lesson to be learned. I went into the room where they were talking.

Me: "Benjamin, you look angry."

Benjamin: "Sure I am. She's wearing my shirt again, and I'm sick of it."

Me: "So it's *her* fault that you're angry?"

Benjamin: "Yes."

Me: "If I gave you a million dollars in cash right now, and a new car of your choice, would you still be angry at Janette?"

Benjamin: (smiling) "Probably not."

Me: "Then it couldn't be *her* fault that you're angry, could it?"

I explained to Benjamin that he was angry only because he felt empty, and in that condition, virtually anything that anyone did made him feel threatened. His anger was just a way to protect himself. A million dollars would make him feel better because it would temporarily make him forget his emptiness. Janette wasn't the problem at all.

Me: "What you really want is to feel loved all the time, but you don't. That's my fault, not Janette's. When she took something of yours without asking, you judged that she didn't care about you — a feeling you've experienced with many people, including me. You hate that feeling, and to protect yourself from it, you got angry. The more loved you feel, the less often you'll have a need to protect yourself by getting angry."

Because Janette didn't feel loved, either, she selfishly used something that didn't belong to her and then defended herself when she was confronted with her mistake.

When both children understood the cause of their anger, and felt loved by me while they were truthful about their selfishness, their anger disappeared. With more love from me, and additional opportunities to see and love each other, they eventually quit having arguments entirely.

Business

In the world of profit and loss, it may seem strange to talk about loving relationships.

The Contract

A contract is an agreement between two or more people about the exchange of goods or services. It is not a relationship. Whereas expectations are destructive in a loving relationship, clear and mutual expectations *are* an accepted part of any contract. For example, as employees, we have a contract with our employer that gives us the right to expect him to pay us for what we do. However, we have no right to expect our employer to give us compassion and love, which are components of a relationship, not a contract.

Larry worked hard to impress his boss. He advertised his successes and always looked busy and cheerful when the boss was around. In addition to his paycheck, he wanted approval and praise. That was a natural but inappropriate desire that resulted from Larry not feeling unconditionally loved all his life. Larry was exhausted by the effort of impressing his employer, and his boss sensed that he was being manipulated and therefore disliked being around Larry.

Without realizing it, most of us expect our employers to "love" us in some way. We prove that when we complain that we're not appreciated or respected, which is another way of saying that we're not loved.

The Relationship

In business, we can have contracts *and* good relationships with the same people.

Harold had the same boss as Larry, but Harold knew he was

loved and worthwhile as a result of telling the truth about himself to several friends who had accepted him unconditionally for a long time. He didn't have the need to manipulate the boss to "love" him and make him feel good. The boss felt the absence of manipulation and therefore enjoyed being around Harold. They had a positive *relationship* in addition to their business contract. When we've received enough Real Love, the effect on all our relationships — even those at work — is profound.

The boss came to work one day in a terrible mood. He snapped at Larry and Harold about something that was not going well on the job.

Because Larry had a need for the boss to make him feel worthwhile, he felt attacked and hurt. He then protected himself from the feeling of being alone and helpless by acting like a victim. He criticized the boss behind his back and denied his part of the responsibility for the problem the boss was complaining about.

Harold already felt loved and worthwhile, so he didn't feel threatened and was able to see the situation clearly. He knew the boss was afraid he'd look bad — and would therefore be less lovable — because of the mistakes that were being made on the job. Harold knew the boss's anger was just an unconscious effort to protect himself from feeling helpless and an attempt to intimidate other people to do what he wanted. Of course, the boss felt accused and attacked by Larry, but seen and accepted by Harold.

In every relationship, even at work, we can learn to see and accept our partners, as Harold did. That's Real Love.

Strangers

Bill often became angry at other drivers as he drove home in heavy traffic.

Bill: "I learned something on my way home from work today. Some guy cut in front of me, and I had to slam on my brakes to keep from hitting him."

Wise man: "What did you do?"

Bill: "I was furious that this fool could be so thoughtless. And I was about to honk the horn and scream at him when I re- membered that every time I'm angry, it's not somebody else's fault. I've learned that my anger is always a reaction to *me* feeling empty and afraid. As I thought about that, I remem- bered that quite a few people — like you — really do love me. And what this man did couldn't change that. His mistake sud- denly became meaningless, and I wasn't angry at him at all."

Wise man: "Felt good, didn't it?"

Bill: "Amazing. I really do have a choice. When I remember that I'm loved, I don't feel angry at anyone. I like having a choice instead of always getting angry and feeling miserable."

We can all learn to see and love people everywhere, even people we only interact with once. Rather than seeing the people around us as an inconvenience when they don't give us what we want, we can learn to see them as an opportunity to be loving.

Chapter Summary

The only worthwhile purpose of all relationships is to get and/or give Real Love. We can learn to tell the truth, feel loved, and love others as we interact with our friends, family members, co-workers, and even strangers.

Chapter 22

Parents and Children

Most parenting books and experts offer techniques for manipulating our children to behave in a way that's convenient for *us*. But good parenting is not a technique, nor is it an opportunity to get something for ourselves. Good parenting is a natural result of teaching and unconditionally loving our children. We become better parents only as we learn to be more loving, not as we learn to make our children do what we want.

Families exist to provide a place where a child can feel unconditionally loved and learn to love others. Of course, children also need to learn the four R's—reading, 'riting, 'rithmetic, and responsibility—but no matter how well they learn those things, if they don't learn how to love other people, they will not be happy. I recommend *The Truth About Parenting* to those interested in a more thorough examination of this subject.

The Responsibility of Children to Love Their Parents

When we don't feel loved ourselves, we unavoidably seek praise, acceptance, and "love" from every available source, including our children. We get "love" from our children in the form of respect, obedience, and gratitude. Those *are* commendable qualities in a child, but a significant part of our motivation for insisting on those virtues is that *our* lives are then more convenient, and we feel more worthwhile as parents. We hate to admit that selfishness, but we prove it every time we get disappointed and angry when our children fail to demonstrate those qualities.

Our demands for love can seem quite innocent, but the effect is still devastating. For example, when a mother says, "Give Mommy a kiss," she unwittingly places on that child the responsibility for loving her. And that's obvious to the child, because she smiles when he kisses her and frowns when he resists. Clearly, he controls her happiness as he chooses whether he'll love her in the way she demands. A child cannot be happy while carrying that burden.

No parent ever has the right to expect love from a child. It's the responsibility of parents to teach and love their children, not the other way around.

Parents Must Feel Loved
Before They Can Love Their Children

During a parenting seminar, a mother approached me with obvious agitation.

Mother: "How do I get my son to stop being angry and rebellious all the time?"

Me: "Children can't be happy while we're trying to '*get*' them to do anything. The whole reason your son is empty and angry is that you've tried to control him instead of loving him unconditionally. And there's no blaming in that — you never had any Real Love to give him. When you feel loved enough yourself, you'll be able to give him what he needs — and then there's a strong possibility that he'll stop being angry and rebellious. Until then, you're helpless to do anything for him."

We want a quick fix for our children, but there isn't one. We must accept the fact that *we* are the primary problem in our children's lives. How could it be otherwise? Who taught our children their values, their fears, and their Getting and Protecting Behaviors? *We* did, but then we want to blame our children's problems on *them*, their peers, the schools, television, etc. Nonsense.

Fortunately, we are more than our children's primary problem. We are also their greatest opportunity for happiness. Children who do feel unconditionally loved by their parents are the happiest creatures on the planet. They simply don't have a need to drink, smoke, yell at their parents, fight with their siblings, act out in school, and have indiscriminate sex. We get to see that proven over and over as we learn to tell the truth about ourselves, feel loved, and learn to give our children the Real Love they require to be happy.

Unconditional Love
Is Not Permissiveness

When I speak about unconditionally loving our children, many people protest: "But somebody has to discipline them. If we don't, how can they learn anything?" Unconditionally loving children does not mean we say and do nothing when they make mistakes. Children do need to be corrected, but they do not need the disappointment and anger which we almost always administer with the instruction we offer. The moment we're irritated, our children correctly sense that we do not love them unconditionally, and the effect is disastrous.

Being permissive with children and controlling them are both destructive approaches. What children need — and what most of us have never seen — is correction that is given with genuine acceptance. That's Real Love.

We Reap What We Sow

There is no job in the world more important than being a parent, but our behavior testifies that we don't believe that. Instead we tend to invest our time and effort in careers, money, entertainment, and impressing other people. The subsequent harvest is a nation of unhappy children whose behaviors are designed to get Imitation Love and protect themselves.

Chapter Summary

More than anything else, children need to be unconditionally loved by
their parents. Without that, children are empty and afraid, and they
respond with the Getting and Protecting Behaviors that make them
miserable and frustrate their parents.

We can't give what we never received. We can only become better
parents when we get Real Love for ourselves.

Chapter 23

God

Imagine communicating by e-mail with a creature who lives on a planet where there is no water. How would you describe water to him? Or the ocean? It's very difficult for anyone to imagine something if they've never experienced anything remotely like it. But if you brought one of those aliens to Earth and sat him beside a stream, he would soon understand a great deal about water, wouldn't he?

Finding a Relationship With God

Similarly, most of us have never seen unconditional love, and that is why we have a confusing relationship — or none at all — with a Being whose most important characteristic is perfect love.

As children, we had no direct, physical contact with God. We therefore learned about Him from the people around us, and one word they commonly used to describe Him was "Father." Unavoidably — and unconsciously — we then assumed that He must be similar to the only other person we knew with that title: our flesh-and-blood father. Because our mortal fathers were often disappointed and angry when we failed to do what they wanted, we naturally concluded that God would feel that way, too. And why would we want to interact with yet another person who criticized us and made us feel unloved? *That* is why many of us don't have a fulfilling relationship with God.

When we begin to feel the unconditional love of wise men and women, it's like seeing our first drop of water. Knowing that water exists, we can begin to imagine an ocean. Feeling unconditional love from a human being, we can begin to imagine a God who offers us an ocean of love. I have been impressed at the consistency of this process. Most people who learn to tell the truth about themselves and find the unconditional love of other people eventually develop a more loving relationship with God.

The Effect of a Relationship With God

"Perfect love casteth out fear." (I John 4:18) When we exercise faith and feel the abundance of God's love, we have never-ending access to the greatest gift of all. With that, there's nothing to fear. Everything we found threatening in the past becomes insignificant. We never have to feel alone again. Without emptiness and fear, seeing and loving other people becomes natural and effortless.

God's Description of Finding Love

For millennia, God has been teaching us how to feel loved and happy: Desire → Faith → Truth → Giving up the Getting and Protecting Behaviors (Chapters 7-11).

Desire and Faith

"Ask, and it shall be given you; seek, and ye shall find; knock, and it shall be opened unto you." (Matthew 7:7) Receiving what we need starts with a sincere desire to find it. And we declare what we really want by what we *do*, not by what we say (Matthew 7:21). We prove our belief that God knows the way to happiness only as we *do* the things He has suggested. Faith without action is nothing (James 2:17, 20).

The Truth

And then we must tell the truth, "... and *the truth shall make you free*." (John 8:31-32) Without the truth, we remain prisoners to confusion and fear.

Giving Up the Getting and Protecting Behaviors

God knows that Imitation Love and our Getting and Protecting Behaviors make it impossible for us to feel loved and happy. Adultery, murder, stealing, envy, drunkenness, and lying are the ways we get praise, power, pleasure, and safety. All of the "thou shalt nots" found in the commandments are simply the directions provided by a deeply loving God to help us stay away from the things that will destroy our happiness. The commandments are not an attempt by an insecure Being to control His children.

Exercising faith and telling the truth, while frightening for moments, are actually *easier* than the never-ending and frustrating effort of manipulating people and protecting ourselves. "My yoke is easy, and my burden is light." (Matthew 10:31)

Choice

God's relationship with us is a natural result of His independent choices and our own. He has chosen to accept and love us. We can now choose to accept His love or reject it. He will never violate our freedom to choose by making us accept Him.

Chapter Summary

As we feel unconditionally loved by other people, we can more easily imagine a relationship with an unconditionally loving God.

God has long described the way to feel loved and happy: Desire → Faith → Truth → Giving up the Getting and Protecting Behaviors.

Obstacles to Love and Solutions

Chapter 24

Role Assignment

"All the world's a stage, and all the men and women merely players." (Shakespeare, *As You Like It*) From the day of our birth, our parents and others teach us the role we will play on the stage of our lives.

Stan's parents taught him the role of The Good Son because they were happier when he played his part well. Stan's biological father played the role of The Father, whose job was to make Stan be obedient, responsible, and successful. When Stan failed to perform his role adequately, The Father punished him with disapproval and anger. Stan's stepmother played The Mother, who complained and acted like a victim to manipulate Stan to love her and take care of her.

Stan eventually became unhappy in this role which required him to constantly please people, but it was the only role he'd ever learned, and he didn't know another way to live. When Stan grew up and moved away, his play became incomplete. How could he be The Good Son and please The Father and The Mother if they weren't there on stage with him? So he found new actors to fill the old roles, and then he was able to return to the familiarity and comfort of the old family play, even though his original family was no longer with him. For the rest of his life, Stan interacted with everyone as though they were the characters in the play he learned as a child.

At work, Stan's supervisor had some of the same character traits as Stan's biological father. With no conscious effort, Stan naturally assigned the role of The Father to his boss. When Stan found some-one to play the role of The Mother, he married her. Everyone in Stan's world was assigned a role in his play.

Even though Stan's supervisor was different in many ways from Stan's father, Stan could only see him in the role of The Father. Stan then reacted to everything the boss said or did as though it were being done by his original father. For example, when the boss offered genu-inely helpful advice, Stan could only hear the critical and angry voice of his father, and then he responded by lying, acting like a victim, and getting angry.

Stan did the same thing with his wife. He treated her as though she *were* The Mother, not just playing a role. He tried to make his wife happy — as he had done with his stepmother — but he also resented her for manipulating him, even when she wasn't doing that.

To varying degrees, *we all do what Stan did*. At an early age, we were compelled to learn a role, and most of us have continued to play that part for the rest of our lives. It's all we know how to do.

We do get some important benefits from playing our role:

1. It minimizes our pain. When we play our part well, people hurt us less. When Stan played The Good Son, for example, his father didn't criticize him, and his stepmother complained less.

2. It maximizes our pleasure. People smile at us more when we're "good" — in other words, when we perform the role they assign us.

3. It gives us a place in the world. Our greatest fear is being alone. Even though our assigned role requires us to satisfy the expectations of other people, it also assures us of relatively predictable interaction with the other characters in our play — and then we feel less alone.

But all these benefits are only forms of Imitation Love. As we play a role, we're always behaving in a way that is designed to win the conditional approval of other people. The moment we do anything to persuade someone to like us, Real Love is impossible (pp. 45-7), and we cannot be genuinely happy.

Interacting Roles

Diane spoke to John in the service department about picking up her car.

Diane: "Is my car ready yet?"

John: "We got it done as fast as we could, lady!!"

Diane burst into tears and stomped off.

What happened here? How could two people who had never met become so upset over such a minor event?

Diane

As a child, Diane was raised by a man who had never felt unconditionally loved. Empty and afraid, he protected himself by being critical and angry with everyone. He defined the role of The Father in Diane's play.

Although it was not intentional, The Father's criticism and anger made Diane afraid and taught her that she was The Stupid Child. When she filled that role, he felt less powerless and afraid. She also learned that when she acted pathetic and tearful — like a victim — he became less angry. Being a victim minimized the pain in her life and gave her a definite place in the world.

For the rest of her life, Diane assigned the role of The Father to most of the men she knew. When they spoke to her critically, she became afraid and reacted by acting like a victim. She often reacted this way even when they were not being critical or angry. This had terrible consequences:

1. With men who really were angry, acting like a victim often minimized their anger, as it had with her father. But the price for that bit of safety was high: she always felt more alone. We can never protect ourselves from someone and at the same time feel closer to them. *All the Protecting Behaviors cause both partners in a relationship to feel more separated and alone* (p. 39).

2. When men were *not* critical or angry, she often assigned them the role of The Father anyway, and reacted as though they *were* angry by acting like a victim. People can only feel like victims when they're blaming someone for their unhappiness, and the people they blame feel that accusation. When Diane acted like a victim, these non-angry men felt her accusation (attack). They reacted by doing one of two things:

> A. They avoided her (running), which made her feel more alone. Of course, the whole reason she acted like a victim in the first place was to attract sympathy so she wouldn't feel alone. It's ironic that our Protecting Behaviors cause the very thing we're trying to avoid.
>
> OR
>
> B. They became angry to defend themselves against Diane's implied accusation. In effect, Diane created anger where there had been none. And again, she felt more alone.

When Diane approached John at the service counter, she assigned him the role of The Father, and she reacted to that *role*, rather than responding to John as an individual. She commonly did that with the men in her life, and it kept her frightened and alone.

John

John's mother constantly manipulated people to get Imitation Love.

She acted like a victim and made people feel guilty for not doing more for her. She defined the role of The Mother in John's play.

The Mother taught John to feel guilty and to serve her when she manipulated him. Although he didn't enjoy the role, when he did it well, he avoided her disappointment and anger. And it gave him a definite place in the world, which made him feel less alone. With time, however, he became increasingly angry to protect himself from the helpless feeling of being controlled by The Mother.

For the rest of his life, John assigned The Mother role to most of the women he knew. When they spoke, he heard the whining and accusation of The Mother, and he reacted with anger, as though these women *were* his real mother. He often did this whether they were actually whining and manipulating him or not. That role assignment had terrible consequences:

1. When women *did* manipulate John, his anger usually frightened them and reduced their complaints. But his anger also kept him alone and unhappy.

2. When women were *not* manipulative, he often treated them as though they were, assigning the Mother role to them. He then protected himself with anger, and they reacted to his anger in one or more of several ways:

    A. They avoided him — they ran. That stopped the manipulation, but it left him feeling alone.

OR

    B. They manipulated him by saying and doing what he wanted, which made him less angry. But their manipulations made a real relationship impossible (pp. 45-7), and again he was alone.

OR

    C. They attacked him with their own anger.

When Diane approached John at the service counter, he saw her as The Mother before she spoke a word. When she said, "Is my car ready **yet**?" he heard the same tone of accusation he heard all his life from The Mother, and he responded with anger: "We got it done as fast as we could, lady!!" It would have been more accurate if he'd said, "I got it done as fast as I could, **Mother!**" All his life, John reacted to women as though they were The Mother, and it kept him angry and alone.

Two Interacting Roles

Both Diane and John were unaware that they had assigned each other a role from the past. But it still happened, and then they couldn't react to the actual person standing in front of them, only to the **role** they had assigned. In effect, John's father and Diane's mother were standing there in the service department confronting each other. It's no wonder that the interaction between John and Diane went poorly — **they** were not really present. This happens with most interactions to varying degrees, and we're largely unaware of it.

We All Do It

How many times have you said something that you thought was innocent, only to have your partner react as though you had attacked them? Or have you wondered why you feel defensive around certain people, even though they've done little or nothing to hurt you? It happens because we assign each other a role from our past, and we react to the role, rather than to each other. This pattern of role assignment makes loving relationships impossible.

As we find unconditional love, we lose the blinding effects of emptiness and fear, and then we can see people as they really are, rather than seeing them as roles from the past. Seeing them clearly, we can accept and love them.

Chapter Summary

Early in life, we were all assigned a role in a play, and we learned to interact with other people who were playing their own roles.

For the rest of our lives, we've continued to play our old role and have assigned to others the roles that came from the original play in which we played a part. This assignment of roles can be very destructive to us and our relationships.

Chapter 25

Eliminating Conflict

As we all practice making our own choices, we unavoidably inconvenience each other. Experts propose ways to "manage" these conflicts, but why should we settle for the superficial and temporary effect of such techniques when we can learn instead to eliminate conflict entirely by filling our lives with unconditional love and genuine happiness?

Real Love

When we feel unconditionally loved, we have everything that matters. Emptiness, fear, and anger are then impossible, and those are the essential ingredients for every conflict. In short, Real Love eliminates conflict, rather than managing or suppressing it.

The Law of Choice

We can all expect to be loved and happy. However, we do *not* have the right to expect any single person or group of people to love us or make us happy. When we do that, we place our own needs above theirs and deny the Law of Choice: "Everyone always has the right to choose what they say and do." (p. 55) When we believe that other people have the right to make their own choices, we don't feel disappointed in them, nor do we get angry when they don't give us what we want. Without anger, the fuel for conflict is gone.

Finding Happiness

We find real happiness when we simply tell the truth about ourselves and let people make their own decisions about accepting and loving us. In the beginning, those loving moments may not come as quickly as we'd like, and they may not come from the people we believe "should" love us — our spouse, parents, children, etc. Fortunately, it doesn't really matter *who* loves us. If we're consistently truthful and follow the steps to finding love (Chapter 7), we *will* attract wise men and women who can see and love us. Real Love from any source has the same miraculous and joyful effect.

We create conflict when we make demands that anyone respond to us in a way that we want. When we do that, we deny their freedom to choose, and what we get won't feel like Real Love. No one finds happiness that way. When we stop making demands of other people, whatever they give us becomes a genuine gift, and that's when we feel unconditionally loved.

We Must Make Our Own Choices

Each year, William traveled to visit his parents during the Christmas holiday. One year he decided to stay home, and his mother was not happy with the news.

Mother: "But you promised! And I've really been counting on your visit."

Throughout their brief conversation, she acted disappointed and offended.

William had a right to make his own choice about where he spent his time. He was not *responsible* for making his mother happy, which does not mean that he didn't *care* about her happiness. We can have a genuine concern for someone's well-being without giving them everything they want. Imagine what it would be like if we had to prove our love for our children by giving them whatever they asked for.

William's mother had never been unconditionally loved, so she constantly manipulated other people to get attention, praise, and a sense of importance. When we're already empty and afraid, every incident where we don't get the Imitation Love we seek becomes a major disappointment. To prevent those disappointments, we try to control other people to give us what we want. Whenever William's mother failed to get the Imitation Love that briefly distracted her from a lifetime of feeling unloved and alone, she experienced the miserable and desperate condition of having neither Real Love nor Imitation Love. That is an intolerable feeling, and it's only natural that she would then express disappointment and pain.

William did not "make" his mother unhappy. He simply gave her an opportunity to feel how empty her life had been for a very long time. Every time we're disappointed or angry, we declare our expectation that someone should abandon their own choices and give us what we want. William's mother did that. When *we* do that, we negatively affect our relationship with that person and further destroy our own happiness.

More Choices

After years of marriage, Carl and Laurie grew tired of their constant arguments. They each found wise men and women to help them tell the truth about themselves and feel loved. As they learned to be loving with each other, they still naturally had occasional conflicts in their interactions.

Laurie was tired and didn't want to prepare the evening meal, so she asked Carl to go out with her to a restaurant. But Carl was also tired and said he preferred to stay home. Instead of having their usual argument, they remembered the Fourth Rule of Seeing (pp. 111-3) and called a wise friend for advice.

Wise man: "This is easy. You can both have what you want. Laurie, you can go out and Carl can stay home."

Laurie: "But I want Carl to go with me."

Wise man: "You don't get to choose what Carl does, only what *you* do. You've indicated that you want three things: (1) to eat a meal you don't have to prepare; (2) to get out of the house for a while; and (3) to spend some time with Carl. You can do all that if you go out, eat by yourself, and then return home to spend the rest of the evening with Carl. Or you could go out and get a meal to bring back and eat with Carl. No problem."

Laurie: "But I want to go out to dinner *with* Carl."

Wise man: "And I'd love to have an extra thousand dollars right now, but does that give me the right to steal it from *you*?"

Laurie: "Of course not."

Wise man: "That's what you're doing with Carl. You believe that if you want something, *he's* obligated to give it to you. That belief will destroy your relationship. We only have the right to make choices about *our* behavior. We can't control the choices of other people to get what we want."

Requests and Expectations

Although expectations are always selfish, we can make requests. The difference between a request and an expectation is *not* a matter of the words we use. One person can make a request with exactly the same words used by another person who is making a demand. True requests are identified by the absence of the disappointment or anger always associated with expectations and demands.

Sometimes our expectations are disguised by the fact that we're simply getting everything we want from our partner. Under those conditions, our disappointment and anger are hidden and reveal themselves only when we don't get what we "request." Laurie thought she was making a request of Carl, but when she didn't get what she wanted, it became obvious that she was making a demand. Eventually, with enough love and practice, we're able to make appropriate and loving requests instead of demands.

It is not appropriate to expect people to do things **for** us, but we can always ask that they stop doing things **to** us. For example, I don't have the right to expect you to love me, but I *can* ask — even insist — that you stop hitting me. However, even if you ignore my request to stop hitting me, I'm never justified in being angry. Anger is always selfish and makes happiness impossible.

A Clever Manipulation

We can turn some requests into clever manipulations and apparently unsolvable conflicts.

As a child, Carl learned to withdraw (run) from threatening experiences. Laurie learned to protect herself by attacking. As adults, they naturally continued to use the same Protecting Behaviors.

What Carl feared most was being criticized, because then he felt worthless and unloved. When he sensed disapproval from Laurie, he quit talking, or went into another room, or spent more time at work — all forms of running. Laurie's greatest fear was feeling unloved and alone, which she always experienced when Carl withdrew from her. To protect herself, she criticized him and made him feel guilty for not spending time with her as a "good husband" should.

Laurie demanded that Carl stop withdrawing from her, and Carl complained that Laurie always criticized him. They were locked in a terribly destructive cycle of protecting themselves, using the very behaviors which frightened their partner the most. Finally, they shared their problem with a wise friend who explained the Law of Choice (p. 55).

Wise man: "Laurie, Carl gets to make his own choices. You don't have the right to demand that he does what you want."

Laurie: "But I do have the right to insist that he stop doing something *to* me, right?"

Wise man: "Yes."

Laurie: "When he withdraws, that hurts me, so he *is* doing something *to* me. And I have the right to tell him to stop it."

Wise man: (smiling) "No, you don't. Using that reasoning, you could force everyone to do whatever you wanted just by saying that you'd be hurt if they didn't give you what you demanded. You could control the whole world with that reasoning. Do you see that?"

Laurie: "But he *does* hurt me when he withdraws. How do I get him to stop it?"

Wise man: "You don't."

The wise man explained the four choices we have in any relationship (pp. 56-63), emphasizing that we don't have the right to change our partner.

Wise man: "In addition, Carl doesn't really hurt you. What you feel is empty and unloved, and that's been going on long before you met Carl. Now you expect him to love you and make up for all the pain from your past. When he doesn't do that, you blame him for the pain you've felt all your life."

Laurie: "So where do I get loved? Isn't that what husbands are for?"

Wise man: "That would be nice, but it's obvious that *neither* of you is capable of loving anyone unconditionally."

The wise man then explained the process of telling the truth about ourselves and finding people capable of loving us unconditionally.

Conflicting Choices vs. Conflicting People

As we learn to feel loved and understand the principle of choice, we can easily deal with conflicting *choices*, rather than suffer the terrible consequences of *people* in conflict.

Carl and Laurie learned how to tell the truth about themselves to loving men and women. As they felt loved and learned to love each other, they still had different preferences about many things: entertainment, food, schedules, etc. That's unavoidable. But when they felt loved, the conflicts were between *choices* and involved no disappointment or anger.

Laurie: "I don't really want to prepare a meal tonight. Can we go out and get something to eat?"

Carl: "I'd love to go with you, but I'm too tired to get out of this chair."

Laurie: "Then I'll go out and get something to bring back for both of us. Is that all right with you?"

Carl: "That would be great. Thanks."

When people care about each other's happiness, it really is that easy to work out a solution for conflicting interests. Loving conversations like this are not the result of learning a technique. Simply saying the "right words" accomplishes nothing when we don't feel loved and loving. Without Real Love, every interaction becomes an exchange of demands for attention and affection, no matter what words we use.

There will always be conflict between choices, priorities, and schedules. But those are just *things*. And in mutually loving relationships, we don't solve such conflicts by winning an argument, giving in, or even compromising. Both partners simply care about each other's happiness when they make decisions, and then conflicts resolve easily.

Controlling other people is selfish and wrong. We are never justified in demanding that our partners do what we want: not when we badly need it; not when they have more than enough to give; and not even when they're married to us.

Chapter Summary

It's inevitable that the choices of two people will sometimes conflict. Such conflicts resolve easily when we feel loved and loving, and when we remember the Law of Choice: we all have the right to make our own choices and never have the right to make other people do what we want.

Chapter 26

Responding to
Getting and Protecting Behaviors

In the absence of Real Love, we use Getting and Protecting Behaviors to feel the brief pleasures of Imitation Love. Even though lying, attacking, acting like victims, and running destroy relationships, most of us still do one or more of those things every day.

What can we do about that? What can we do when we find ourselves once again using those behaviors which can only make us unhappy? When we remember that Getting and Protecting Behaviors are only reactions to the absence of Real Love, the solution is obvious: we need to tell the truth about ourselves and create the opportunity to feel unconditionally accepted. As we feel loved, we simply have no need for Getting and Protecting Behaviors.

Responding to getting and protecting *in other people* is also very simple when we feel loved and when we remember that anything we do to protect ourselves or to get people to like us makes a loving relationship impossible (pp. 45-7). When we eliminate all those behaviors, we're left with one productive response to Getting and Protecting Behaviors in others: telling the truth about ourselves.

In short, *telling the truth about ourselves is the solution* to all situations where Getting and Protecting Behaviors arise, whether in ourselves or in others. That approach creates opportunities for us to feel accepted and loved, and it's also very reassuring to other people when they're empty and afraid. I'll go through each of the Getting and Protecting Behaviors now and illustrate how this approach works.

Our Own Lies

Most of us lie every day. Whenever we hide who we really are, we're lying. We lie to protect ourselves and to make people like us. Ironically, our lies make us feel unloved and alone, the worst feeling of all — and most of us don't know how to stop.

Andrew often ate lunch with his co-workers. They were all athletes and outdoorsmen, so they usually talked about things like sports and hunting. Because Andrew had little experience with those things, he rarely spoke.

Andrew mentioned to a wise friend that he felt uncomfortable with the men at work.

Wise man: "That's because you're lying to them."

Andrew: "Lying? How?"

Wise man: "When they talk about football, do you admit that you don't know much about it, or that you've never been to a game?"

Andrew: "Well, no."

Wise man: "When you hide the truth about yourself, you're lying. And the moment you lie, you can't feel accepted by the people you're with."

Andrew: "But if I tell them how little I know about the things they like, they'll think I'm stupid."

Wise man: "You *are* stupid, at least about sports. We're all stupid about lots of things. Do you feel comfortable around me?"

Andrew: "Yes."

Wise man: "But I love sports, just like the men you work with. You feel accepted by me because you chose to tell me the truth about yourself. If you had lied to me, you wouldn't feel comfortable around me, either."

Andrew: "If I tell the truth to the guys at work, they might not accept me like you have."

Wise man: "That's true. Some of them might not. On the other hand, as long as you lie to them, you won't ever feel accepted by *any* of them."

We can only feel loved when people accept us as we really are. They can't do that until *we* tell the truth and allow them to see us. The only way to overcome our fear of telling the truth about ourselves is to simply do it. On the other hand, we don't have to tell people everything about ourselves, and we don't have to start with the people we fear the most: our co-workers, some family members, etc. (pp. 107-8)

The Lies of Others

People lie to us for the same reasons we lie to them. Their primary intent is not to cause us harm, but to get Imitation Love and protect themselves. Unfortunately, when people lie, they always feel more empty and miserable. As we lovingly help people see their lies, we create opportunities for them to feel accepted and loved.

Unfortunately, we rarely confront people about their lies for *their* benefit. When people lie, we tend to feel offended or betrayed, so we confront them with the truth to protect ourselves or because it gives us a sense of power over them. When we tell people the truth without being unconditionally loving, or when they're not capable of hearing the truth about themselves, we can only hurt them, and we need to keep our observations to ourselves (pp. 162-3).

Even on the occasions when we are loving, it is often useful to remember the guideline that telling the truth about *ourselves* is a good approach in responding to all Getting and Protecting Behaviors.

Beth had arranged to have lunch with a wise friend, Martha.

Martha: "You seem upset."

Beth: "I'm really mad at my boss. No matter what I do, he finds something wrong with it. Today he filed a written complaint about me, and I could lose my job if he does it again. It's completely unfair, because none of it was my fault."

Martha had known Beth a long time, and she knew that Beth always acted like a victim and blamed everyone around her instead of being responsible for her own laziness and bad attitude — on the job or anywhere else. But Martha loved Beth and accepted her completely, even when she lied about her mistakes. Martha also knew that Beth could never change her life until she started telling the truth about herself.

Martha: "Sounds bad. This must have been going on for a long time between the two of you."

Beth: "Yes, it has. He's always had something against me."

Martha: (laughing) "Over the years, I've had some bosses that I just couldn't get along with, either. And I've learned one thing about all of them. No matter what they did, in every single case, I always did something — usually a lot of things — that made the situation worse. If the boss didn't appreciate me, for example, I talked about him behind his back. If he told me to do things that I didn't agree with, I did what he wanted as slowly as I could, which just made him more angry at me. Each of those people may not have been perfect, but I was a big part of the problem every time."

Beth was stunned, obviously expecting Martha to sympathize with her and agree that her boss was a monster. After several seconds of silence, Martha continued by giving even more examples of her selfishness as an employee, showing how that had caused tension between herself and her employers and co-workers. The more Martha talked, the more relaxed Beth became.

Beth: "Okay, okay, I get the point. I haven't been the model employee. I don't like my boss one bit, and I haven't exactly hidden that fact."

Beth then talked about many things she'd done to make her boss's job more difficult, and she saw how *she* had caused her own problems at work. After several conversations like that with Martha, Beth apologized to her boss for all the trouble she had caused for many months. He was surprised and pleased by her honesty, and their relationship improved considerably.

We can all learn how to tell people about their lies in a loving way. Obviously, the first requirement is that we feel loved ourselves. For more about how to tell people the truth about them, see *The Wise Man*.

Attacking

Any time we attempt to motivate people through fear to do what we want, we're attacking them. Criticism and anger are common forms of attacking.

The Criticism of Others

It is possible to offer loving criticism, but most of the time when we criticize someone, we do it to protect ourselves or to achieve a sense of importance and power.

Becky called her parents to describe the house she had just purchased. Her father responded by telling her about the many mistakes she'd made: the property values were declining in that neighborhood; the interest rate on the bank loan was too high; the house was too old; etc. Becky felt stupid and unloved, as she always had as a child.

Becky had an impulse to act like a victim or to get angry at her father for not accepting her, but instead she called a wise friend who encouraged her to tell the truth about herself. Becky admitted that she didn't know much about real estate and had made several mistakes in the process of buying her house. She also acknowledged that she still felt unsure of being loved, and in that condition, almost any criticism was enough to be very threatening to her. That was *her* problem, not her father's fault. As she told the truth about herself, she felt accepted and loved by her wise friend, and her anger vanished.

When people criticize us, we tend to protect ourselves, which is foolish because we never feel loved and happy when we use Protecting Behaviors. It's ironic that real safety is only achieved when we abandon Getting and Protecting Behaviors and simply tell the truth about ourselves.

When we feel loved, we can see that critical people are just afraid and protecting themselves. We can then accept them instead of fearing them and defending ourselves. Becky's father was not intentionally malicious. He had just never been unconditionally loved himself. He had learned over the years that he temporarily felt less worthless and alone when he appeared to know a lot and gave people advice. Unfortunately, his approach was always condescending and critical, so he alienated himself from everyone.

Our Own Anger

We're disappointed and angry at people so often that we accept it as normal. With our exasperated sighs, disapproving shakes of the head, tone of voice, and rolling eyes, we demonstrate our selfish belief that other people should never be an inconvenience to us. Anger destroys relationships, and more important, it always makes *us* unhappy.

Edward was irritated at his wife, Amanda.

Edward: "Everywhere we go, she's late. It's so rude."

Wise man: "Do *you* ever make mistakes?"

Edward: "Of course, but I'm not late all the time."

Wise man: "Although you may possess the virtue of punctuality in great abundance, you do have other faults which unavoidably inconvenience people on occasion, probably more often than you realize. And that's how it has to be. We must be allowed to make our own mistakes. That's how we learn. Does Amanda have the same right to make mistakes that you do?"

Edward: (long pause) "I never thought about that."

As Edward began to see the selfishness of his anger, his irritation faded. It's difficult to stay angry and blaming when we see how unloving it is.

Edward: "So what do I do about Amanda being late?"

Wise man: "Do you want to divorce her over this?"

Edward: "No."

Wise man: "Then you only have two choices left (pp. 58-63). You can accept her and love her *while she continues to be late* **or** you can keep being angry at her. If you choose to accept her, you'll have a loving relationship with a delightful woman who also happens to be late on some occasions. If you choose to resent her, you can only be unhappy. So what's your choice, to be happy or unhappy?"

Edward: "You make it look like such an easy decision."

Wise man: "It is."

Edward: "I want to be happy, obviously, but does that mean that she gets to keep being late?"

Wise man: "Of course. She gets to learn the same way you do — by making mistakes. And it's impossible to make mistakes without inconveniencing other people — in this case, *you*. If you genuinely care about her happiness, her being late will matter very little to you. Right now, however, your anger demonstrates that you don't feel loved enough to genuinely care about her happiness. You care more about your own convenience, and that's natural until you feel more loved."

As Edward felt accepted, he saw the truth of what his friend was saying.

Blaming and anger protect us from feeling helpless, but that never makes us feel loved or happy. What we really need is to tell the truth about ourselves and create opportunities to be unconditionally accepted and loved. As we feel loved, we lose our emptiness and fear, along with the anger that is only a reaction to those feelings.

Several days after the above conversation, Edward called.

Edward: "Amanda was late again. I know it's selfish, but I'm still angry about it."

Wise man: "I was angry most of my life. But I learned to tell the truth about myself and found people who accepted me. As I felt loved, my expectations and anger gradually disappeared. The same will happen for you. And right now, you're doing the best thing you could be doing: you're telling the truth about your own selfishness. How does that feel?"

Edward: "I don't think I've ever felt accepted by someone while I was admitting that I was selfish and stupid. I like this."

Edward had felt unloved all his life, and each time his wife was late, he saw that as more evidence that nobody cared about him. His anger gave him some relief from the feeling of being alone and helpless. What he really needed was to feel accepted, and his wise friend provided that.

The Anger of Others

After a shower, Edward left the bathroom a mess, and Amanda was angry about it. As she nagged him, his first impulse was to attack her by describing all the times she made messes herself. And then he thought about just leaving the room and refusing to talk to her (running). He had considerable experience with both approaches. But this time he remembered a conversation with his wise friend where he admitted that defending himself had never made him happy.

Edward knew he couldn't open his mouth without saying something unkind, so he said, "Excuse me, I have to go and make a phone call. But I'll be right back to finish this discussion with you." Edward then called his wise friend.

Edward: "Amanda is yelling at me, and I don't know what to do.

Instead of blowing up at her and getting into a big fight, I stopped what I was doing to call you."

Wise man: "You're getting pretty smart. You already know you can't demand that *she* change in any way. That never works. But there is something you can do that involves only you. You can tell the truth about yourself."

Edward: "About what? That I'm feeling unappreciated and angry?"

Wise man: "Yes. Let's start with 'angry.' It's important that you feel accepted *while* you're angry. But as you know, expressing your anger to Amanda wouldn't work very well."

Edward: "That's why I called you."

Wise man: "Very wise. How are you feeling right now?"

Edward: "Getting loved always feels good. I didn't feel that way when Amanda was yelling at me."

Wise man: "Now let's talk about something a little harder. You said you were feeling 'unappreciated.' When Amanda attacked you, you became afraid, and after that you immediately began to protect yourself, at least in your head. Your anger is a form of attacking, one of the Protecting Behaviors. What Protecting Behavior are you using with the word 'unappreciated?'"

Edward: "I don't think I like seeing that very much. I was being a victim."

Wise man: "Of course you were. Don't feel ashamed about it. Just see the truth of it. Now don't stop there. If you were attacking with anger and being a victim — even though it was just silently this time — what is the likelihood that you were feeling loving toward Amanda?"

Edward: "Zero."

Wise man: "Exactly. You were being angry and unloving toward your own wife. It doesn't get much more selfish and ugly than that. And yet here you are being absolutely honest about it, something that very few people on the planet can do. I think you're amazing. How do you feel now?"

Edward: "I'd rather spend the rest of the day here than go back and talk to Amanda."

Wise man: "Take all the time you need. When you feel loved enough, you can go back and tell the truth about yourself to Amanda instead of getting into another useless argument. You won't believe what a relief it is to just say that you were wrong."

Edward: "But all I did was leave a little mess in the bathroom. Does that justify her yelling at me?"

Wise man: "No, it doesn't, but we're not here to talk about her, just you. Do you want to blame her and have an argument or learn how to be loving and happy? It seems to me that you already know how to blame and argue. Why not learn something new?"

Edward: "Good point."

Wise man: "Was it thoughtless of you to leave a mess in the bathroom?"

Edward: "Well yes, but . . ."

Wise man: "There is no 'but.' You were thoughtless and selfish. If you really cared about Amanda, you wouldn't have left that mess. True?"

Edward: "I guess so."

Wise man: "Now if you feel loved enough, go and tell the truth to Amanda."

Edward: "I think I can do that. It helps a lot that I could talk to you and feel accepted before I talk to her."

Wise man: "Oh, I know. I had to do this with friends a million times before I quit arguing with my wife. But now we don't argue about anything anymore. It's a lot more fun this way, I can tell you."

Edward told Amanda that he had been thoughtless and wrong. She was dumbfounded and responded by apologizing for being so unkind toward him. It was a turning point in their relationship.

People are only angry because they're empty and afraid. When we defend ourselves, they feel even more afraid and use their Protecting Behaviors more vigorously. And on it goes. We can stop all that by simply telling the truth about ourselves. When one or both parties in a disagreement admits to being wrong, it's difficult to continue the argument. As we practice telling the truth and feeling loved, we can actually be loving toward people who are attacking us.

Victimhood

Victimhood is the result of our belief that other people have an obligation to make choices that will benefit us. It's a combination of anger (that we don't get more than we have) and fear (that we'll be hurt).

The cry of the victim is, "Look what you did **to** me," as well as, "Look what you should have done **for** me." Victims assume that the first choice of every human being should be to give them what they want. When that doesn't happen, life is unfair.

Lori and Phil had been married for ten years and had two children.

Lori: "You never spend any time with me."

Phil: "I do things with you all the time. And you never appreciate it. Whatever I do, it's never enough."

Both Lori and Phil were being victims. Lori believed that Phil was obligated to satisfy her needs and spend all the time with her that she wished. Phil believed that Lori should always appreciate him and never have expectations of him or misunderstand him. They both chose to act wounded after not getting what they expected.

It's difficult to have a relationship with a victim. They see everything being done *to* them or *for* them. They see people as *things* that will either make them happy or hurt them. They don't have relationships with people, just with objects they use.

The solution for being a victim — and for reacting to one — is the same as for lying and attacking. We need to tell the truth about ourselves and get loved. It's impossible to feel loved and feel victimized at the same time.

Lori met with two wise friends for lunch and told them about her interactions with Phil. They knew that Lori didn't need sympathy — she needed to be seen clearly and accepted. They told her she was being selfish and demanding, and because Lori could feel that they accepted and loved her, she listened and admitted that she was wrong. It feels wonderful to be accepted while we're doing something wrong.

Over a period of months, Lori continued to tell the truth about herself to wise friends. As she felt more loved, she was eventually able to tell Phil that she had been selfish and ungrateful toward him for a long time. Phil didn't feel attacked anymore and quit withdrawing from her. Their relationship changed dramatically.

Running

We run to protect ourselves. When we withdraw physically and emotionally from people, we're running. When we drink alcohol and take drugs, we're running. Andrew's silence (pp. 220-1) was a form of running, in addition to lying.

The solution is the same as for all Getting and Protecting Behaviors. When someone withdraws from us, we need to tell the truth about ourselves, often to someone other than the person withdrawing from us. As we feel loved, we can offer acceptance and love to the person who is running. When people feel our love, they no longer have a need to run from us.

The Reward

As we tell the truth about ourselves and feel unconditionally loved, the happiness we experience is like nothing else. It makes all the money, power, praise, sex, and other forms of entertainment the world has to offer seem like worthless garbage. In addition, as we feel loved ourselves, we can love those around us, and *most* people respond very positively to that. With Real Love, they become less empty and afraid, so they lose their need to use Getting and Protecting Behaviors.

But some people don't respond positively to being loved. After a lifetime of being hurt, they're just too afraid, and they continue to protect themselves even when they're offered what they really need. Despite *their* negative reaction, *we* are always happier when we're loved and loving. Loving other people is always the best way to live.

Occasionally, when we're empty and afraid, we return to the familiarity of Getting and Protecting Behaviors. Praise, power, pleasure, and safety give us temporary relief from our pain and loneliness. We don't need to wallow in guilt about our mistakes. We just need to start telling the truth about ourselves again and feel the acceptance and love that are always available to us.

Chapter Summary

We only use Getting and Protecting Behaviors when we're empty and afraid. The same is true of other people. The only way to break out of the habit of using those behaviors, and the only productive way to respond to them in others, is to simply tell the truth about ourselves to people capable of accepting and loving us. As we feel loved, the need to protect ourselves and to get Imitation Love vanishes.

Chapter 27

The End of a Relationship
(Including Divorce)

Any two people can have a loving relationship if they tell the truth about themselves. However, some people are so emotionally crippled by years of feeling empty and afraid that they're either unable or unwilling to tell the truth. We may need to consider whether it's wise to continue a relationship with such a person.

Making a Choice and
Accepting the Choices of Others

If we had unlimited time, we could pursue a relationship with everyone we met. But time is limited and precious, and we naturally want to fill it with as much knowledge, love, and happiness as we can. We must therefore make decisions constantly about establishing, continuing, and ending relationships.

People really get to make their own choices, even if they choose to lie, protect themselves, and be miserable. And we can still accept them and care about their happiness while they do those things. However, when someone chooses to lie consistently, they can't give or receive Real Love, which is the whole purpose of a relationship (p. 56). By definition, such a person has chosen to not participate in a loving relationship with us, and when we leave that relationship, we're simply accepting their decision.

I'm not suggesting we give up on every relationship where someone tells a lie. Virtually everyone does that occasionally. However, when someone habitually refuses to tell the truth — especially if they attack us and worsen the emptiness and fear we already have — continuing that relationship may not only be unproductive, but may interfere with our own ability to tell the truth, feel loved, and learn to love others. It's simply best that some relationships end.

Loving and Leaving

We can care about someone's happiness unconditionally (Real Love) and still choose to not spend time with them. I introduced this subject on p. 151.

After learning to tell the truth about herself, Joanne began to feel loved and slowly gained the ability to love other people. Joanne had two long-time friends who wanted nothing to do with telling the truth. They constantly talked about people behind their backs, got angry, acted like a victims, and manipulated people for approval. When they did those things with Joanne, because she was still unfamiliar with feeling and giving Real Love, she forgot how loved she felt with wise men and women and became empty and afraid. Of course, she then returned to the use of Getting and Protecting Behaviors of her own. Joanne finally realized that her relationship with these old friends was not helping anyone, and it was actually hurting *her*. So she quit associating with them, even though she continued to care about her friends' happiness.

When to Say Good-Bye

The only way to discover whether someone will tell the truth and experience Real Love is to keep loving them and see what happens. Almost everyone resists the truth about themselves in the beginning. If we abandon every relationship when someone lies or protects themselves, we'll have no relationships at all.

However, some people consistently refuse to tell the truth, and each of us has to decide whether it's worth continuing a relationship with such a partner. How much time and effort do we spend before choosing to give up? We learn the answer to that as we get loved ourselves and learn how to love others. And we learn from making many mistakes.

One winter, I hiked with a friend far out in the desert. Going upstream, we walked and swam across a river many times as it ran between the high canyon walls. The water was so cold that chunks of ice floated in it, and we had to build fires several times to regain the feeling in our legs.

We prepared poorly for our trip. We didn't take sufficient clothing, food, or other supplies. And we had no map, only vague instructions from someone who had walked downstream in the summertime, when the water was warm. We were told that eventually we'd come to a small cabin where we could rest and thaw out.

The hike became a nightmare. In many places, the ice extended from one canyon wall to the other, and we were able to continue only by breaking the ice with our legs and arms. Our progress was slow and painful. After pressing on far into the night of the second day, we had still not reached the cabin, and we were hungry, freezing, and out of food. We finally gave up and made camp, exhausted and shivering. It was a miserable night. We slept so close to the fire that we woke up repeatedly to extinguish the flames that were consuming our sleeping bags.

When we awoke the next morning, we could not believe what we saw: there was the cabin, across the stream less than a hundred yards away. If we had walked two more minutes the night before, we'd have eaten a hot meal and slept in warm beds!

Similarly, it's tragic to give up on a relationship that could have been unspeakably rewarding if we had just put a little more love and effort into it. On the other hand, some relationships cannot be made healthy and need to be abandoned. We're not obligated to spend our lives with every person we meet. We all have to choose where our time is spent most wisely.

Making Decisions About Relationships
Without Long-Term Commitment

When we understand the importance of telling the truth and sharing Real Love, we can make decisions about spending time with people fairly quickly after meeting them. If a potential partner is manipulative and obviously resists telling the truth about himself, why try to make him into something he isn't? We usually need to move on to people who are more interested in telling the truth about themselves and finding Real Love.

Jeff had been learning to tell the truth about himself and to feel accepted and loved by a group of wise men for more than a year. One day, he spoke to a friend and said that he was thinking of marrying Julia, the woman he'd been dating for the last four months.

Jeff: "But I'm still inexperienced at judging unconditional love — especially where women are involved — and I want your opinion. How can I be sure that this is the right woman for me?"

Wise man: "Are you sleeping with her?

Jeff: "No. I have learned *some* things from talking with you guys — and from my own experiences."

Wise man: "That was a good decision. Describe her."

Jeff: "She's beautiful, charming, witty, and has more talents than you can count. We also share lots of interests in common and have a great time together."

Wise man: "Do you want to be loved by your spouse or be entertained by her?"

Jeff: "No contest. I'd rather be loved."

Wise man: "Think about all the positive qualities you listed when I asked you to describe Julia: beautiful, witty, talented, etc. Is that a description of someone who is unconditionally loving, or someone who would entertain you?"

Jeff: "Until you asked, I never thought about it that way. I guess it doesn't have much to do with unconditional love. But I do care about her happiness."

Wise man: "I believe you. I've known you for over a year now, and you've learned a lot about feeling loved and caring about other people. But now you also want a relationship with someone who is capable of caring about *you*, don't you?"

Jeff: "Sure."

Wise man: "I can't tell you whether this particular woman is the one for you. That's really none of my business, in fact. But I can tell you what I suggest to everyone who is seriously dating and looking for a lifelong partner. If I had to pick only one quality that I wanted most in a potential spouse, it would be this: 'Can he or she easily admit being wrong?'"

Jeff: "Explain that."

Wise man: "People can't learn to be loving when they can't admit they're wrong. We can't *learn* anything if we're already *right* about everything. If a person is willing to be wrong, they can learn anything, including how to participate in a mutually loving relationship, and that's what you're looking for isn't it?"

Jeff: "Yes."

Wise man: "So the important question to ask about her is this: what
          happens when you disagree about something, like when you
          don't want to go where she wants or when you don't want to
          do what she wants to do?"

Jeff: "I hadn't really thought about our relationship that way. I was
          just trying to have a good time. (long sigh) She does have a
          definite tendency to get irritated, or sulk, when she doesn't
          get her way. In fact, I usually avoid any kind of disagreement
          with her. I just give in, I'm embarrassed to say."

Wise man: "Have you talked to her about the things you're learning,
          like telling the truth about yourself and feeling unconditionally
          accepted?"

Jeff: "Yes, but she doesn't seem interested in that stuff. When I talk
          about my mistakes, past and present, she seems uncomfort-
          able, and she never talks about hers. She doesn't like to be
          wrong. If there's a disagreement, she's always right and gets
          her way. But I figured with all her other positive qualities, we
          could still have a great relationship."

Wise man: "Have you had other relationships with women who were
          fun and beautiful like Julia?"

Jeff: "Sure."

Wise man: "And did any of those relationships become what you were
          looking for in a marriage?"

Jeff: (smiling) "No, and I'm finally understanding what you're get-
          ting at. I was about to make the same mistake with this woman
          that I made with the others. I even married one of them. It's

fun to be with beautiful and talented women, but that kind of excitement never lasts. So what do I do now?"

Wise man: "Do you think that in the near future, Julia will develop an interest in telling the truth about herself and learning about unconditional love?"

Jeff: "No, I think she's already made that pretty clear."

Wise man: "Then I suggest that you wave good-bye and run like the wind. Putting off your separation won't benefit either of you. But this is all just my opinion. It's obviously your decision to make."

Jeff didn't need another superficial relationship filled with Imitation Love. He needed more practice telling the truth, feeling loved, and learning to love others. He followed the advice of the wise man and immediately ended his relationship with Julia. When he talked to her, he took all the responsibility for the break-up himself, saying that he was simply not loving enough yet to be in a serious relationship.

When we're learning to find Real Love, we don't need any relationships that fail to contribute to that goal. However, the decision to give up on a relationship is quite different when there's a long-term commitment involved, like with a spouse or family member.

Divorce

Marriage is a relationship where we commit to stay with our partner even when they lie, attack, act like a victim, or run (Chapter 19). Marriage is probably the greatest opportunity we have to learn how to love another person. I've seen truly horrible marriages change as the partners honored their commitment to stay together while they learned to tell the truth and love each other.

However, a relationship naturally results from the choices people make independently (p. 55). Sometimes one or both partners in a marriage make choices that eliminate the possibility of a loving relationship.

Cynthia's husband frequently hit her when he was drunk, and he drank almost every day. She lived with that for years, requiring hospitalization on two occasions for her injuries. She found it impossible to learn to tell the truth and find Real Love in that environment.

She finally divorced her husband and moved to another city. She found a group of wise women, learned to tell the truth, and felt the effect of Real Love for the first time in her life. She became very happy and married a man who loved her unconditionally.

People were thrilled for Cynthia. No one doubted that she had made the right choice in leaving her abusive husband.

Michael's wife was an angry, bitter woman who had something critical and hateful to say every time she opened her mouth. For many years, he tried to please her, but he always failed. He became depressed and developed high blood pressure. He felt so attacked and afraid that he couldn't imagine telling the truth about himself or ever being happy.

He divorced his wife and moved to another city. He found a group of wise men, learned to tell the truth, and felt loved for the first time in his life. He became very happy and married a woman who loved him unconditionally.

Oddly, most people were not as happy for Michael as they were for Cynthia. They accused him of irresponsibly abandoning his wife. The terrible injuries to Michael were less evident than Cynthia's bruises, but they were not less painful or deadly. He never required hospitalization, but his life was no less threatened.

There is no blaming here of Cynthia's husband or Michael's wife. They had never been unconditionally loved themselves, and in that condition, they naturally chose to protect themselves and get Imitation Love, making a loving relationship with their spouses impossible. When Cynthia and Michael left, they were simply accepting the choices already made by their partners.

Most people without Real Love find it very difficult to start telling the truth about themselves and begin the process of feeling accepted and loved. In a sufficiently hostile environment — as with an angry and manipulative spouse — that learning process becomes virtually impossible. This doesn't make their unhappiness the *fault* of the unloving partner. However, people who feel unloved do need a place where they're not surrounded by accusing and blaming, where they can feel relatively safe and free to tell the truth. Most people can find such a place without leaving their marriage, but some cannot.

Abandoning any relationship is not a small thing. Leaving a marriage is a monumental decision. Where possible, I suggest not making such a decision while we're afraid and protecting ourselves. Under those conditions, we can't see anything clearly, and we can't know who or what the real problem is.

If you're empty, angry, offended, blaming, or running, don't make hasty or final decisions. Instead tell the truth, get loved, and learn to love others. When you feel more loved and loving, you'll see clearly and will know the right thing to do. Alice wisely took that approach (pp. 172-3).

Before considering a divorce, also ask yourself, "Have I done all I can do?" That doesn't mean you've done all that *anyone* could do, only all that *you* can do. Have you told the truth about yourself to people who accepted and loved you? Have you learned to love others so you could bring that quality back to the relationship with your partner? Or did you just blame everything on your spouse, eager to leave a difficult situation?

If we don't do all that we can to become loving, we'll repeat the same mistakes in the next relationship and will likely fail at that one, too. If we make our present partner responsible for our unhappiness, we'll do that with the next one. We need to take responsibility for our own feelings and behavior. In most cases, when we leave a committed relationship, we're leaving because *we* are not sufficiently loving.

Temporary Separation

Some of the most unloving relationships can change. Sometimes people need to be away from their partner only temporarily, where they can learn more easily in a safer and less confusing place. When they've learned to tell the truth and feel loved, they can bring that love back to their relationship, which can then change dramatically.

Once Last Comment

In spite of all this talk about leaving relationships, sometimes staying in a relationship with an unloving partner is simply the right thing to do. That partner may be a friend or even a spouse. They may never learn to tell the truth, or accept our love, or love us in any way. But we can learn to love *them* and find great happiness in doing that. I have enjoyed many richly rewarding relationships with friends who never learned a single thing about Real Love.

Chapter Summary

Some people have been empty and afraid for so long that they simply can't or won't tell the truth. They can't feel loved and can't participate in a loving relationship.

We need to consider whether it's wise to continue a relationship with such a person. We need to think about that very seriously and do all we can to change ourselves before we terminate a relationship with a spouse.

Exercises and Stuff

Chapter 28

Our Lies and
What We're Really Saying

For reasons we've discussed, we lie a great deal — and mostly unconsciously. When we do, the consequences are severe: we can't feel loved or participate in loving relationships. For that reason, we need to learn to identify our lies. Only then can we give them up.

This chapter contains just a few of the many lies we tell, along with the truth we lack the courage or insight to express. I suggest talking with a friend about how you tell each of these lies — in various ways and situations — to the people in your life. Then practice telling the truth. This simple activity creates wonderful opportunities to be seen and accepted.

The chapter will be organized in the following way for each lie:

The Lie we tell

The Truth as experienced wise men and women would communicate it to each other. Most of us are not able to tell the truth as boldly as suggested after each lie. That takes practice, and we'll get that practice as we discuss the following lies and tell the truth with a friend. With some of the lies, more than one version of the truth is offered, since people may have different reasons for telling the same lie.

Discussion

Nothing to Lose

In the beginning, it's understandable that most of us are afraid to be honest about ourselves. However, because lying *always* makes us feel unloved and alone — the worst feelings of all — what do we really have to lose by telling the truth? Nothing. If we tell the truth about ourselves and someone rejects us, that person obviously wasn't capable of unconditionally loving us anyway. The only way to create a genuinely loving relationship is to simply tell the truth. So let's examine and eliminate all the lies we can.

"The traffic was bad."

We tend to give this answer — or a similar excuse — when asked why we were late to a meeting or other event. It's one of many ways to say, "It wasn't my fault."

The Truth

"Obviously, I didn't think this meeting was important, or I would have been here on time. If I had really wanted to avoid being late, I would have gotten up much earlier than I did and would have planned to be here long before the meeting started. And clearly, I didn't care about you personally, either, because I wasted your time by making you wait for me."

Discussion

I do not suggest that we all tell the complete truth — as above — the next time we're late for a meeting. It would be a bit overwhelming for most employers and co-workers. However, we *can* be completely honest with a friend, and we can practice being increasingly honest with others.

I was a guest on a radio show when a caller asked some questions about learning to tell the truth. I said that the more honest he could be about himself, the more accepted and loved he would feel.

Caller: "I don't see how this could possibly work on the job. Do you have any suggestions?"

Me: "Sure. When you go to work tomorrow, you'll discover that in no time at all, you'll have an opportunity to tell a lie. Someone will probably confront you with a mistake that you've made. Before that happens, promise yourself that you'll tell the truth instead of making an excuse or blaming someone else — which is lying."

He said he'd try it, and he called me several days later to say that sure enough, the very next morning after the radio show he was five minutes late for the first staff meeting of the day. Everyone in the room looked at him accusingly, and just as he was about to say, "The traffic was bad," he remembered our conversation and his promise. So he stopped, took a deep breath, and in front of everyone, said this: "I was thoughtless and planned my morning poorly. That's why I'm late. I have no good excuse. Next time I'll be more considerate."

He said that everyone looked at him like he'd taken off his pants. And he did feel a little naked without the protection of the usual excuse. But after the meeting, several people said positive things to him because of what he'd said about being late. And his *boss* said this: "In all the years I've worked with employees, I've heard just about every excuse you can imagine. They bore me to death. I *love* what you said this morning. Thank you." The caller went on to say that he felt a real sense of relief when he didn't lie that morning, and it continued throughout the day. He also noticed that the people in the meeting treated him differently after that. Most people really like it when we're honest with them.

"I love you."

The Truth

"Really loving you would mean caring about *your* happiness, but I care a lot more about how *I* feel. I like it when you do what *I* want. When you listen to me, I feel flattered and important. When you spent time with me, I don't feel as empty and alone. I feel good when I'm with you."

Discussion

When we don't feel unconditionally loved and we tell someone we love them, we're only expressing a selfish wish for that person to keep making *us* feel good. But when we say "I love you," our partner hears us promise that we'll make *them* happy. Those conflicting expectations cause the failure of most relationships.

Loving relationships are not created by saying "I love you," no matter how many times we say it. Real Love grows from telling the truth about ourselves and finding those who are capable of accepting us. As we feel loved ourselves, we can eventually say, "I love you" in a genuine and effortless way.

"I'm sorry."

We're often in a position to express regret about something thoughtless and unkind we did which inconvenienced or hurt someone else.

The Truth

"I hate it that you caught me being selfish. Now I can't hide the fact that I did what I wanted and didn't care about your needs or how you'd feel when I did this."

Discussion

We often use apologies to protect *ourselves* rather than to express genuine regret for inconveniencing someone else. With rare exceptions, if we really didn't want to inconvenience someone, we wouldn't do it in the first place.

Me: "Joseph, I see the garbage wasn't taken out this morning."

Joseph: "I'm sorry."

Years before this particular event, I would have been angry and criticized his irresponsibility. And he would have apologized not because he genuinely regretted his laziness, but to escape my anger. Most of us apologize for the same reason. As I learned to teach and love my children, I acquired the ability to continue the conversation past "I'm sorry."

Me: "*Why* was the garbage not taken out?"

Joseph: "I didn't have time. I had to go to school."

Me: "What time did you get up this morning?"

Joseph: "7:00."

Me: "Did you have time to eat? Get dressed? Comb your hair?"

Joseph: "Yes, but . . ."

Me: "Today has twenty-four hours in it, just like yesterday and the day before, and we all make choices about how we'll use that time. You chose to get up at a time that made it impossible to get ready for school *and* take out the garbage. If you had gotten up ten minutes earlier, could you have taken out the garbage?"

Joseph: "Yes."

Joseph's initial "I'm sorry" didn't mean much, which is the case with most apologies. A genuine apology means we regret our behavior and strongly intend to not repeat what we did. It's also a declaration that we are *wrong*. But Joseph didn't claim responsibility for being wrong. Instead, he blamed a lack of time. As long as he believed his behavior was justified in any way, he would never have a reason to change it.

We talked until he saw that the problem was not time, but *his choices*. He was able to listen without resentment only because we had shared many previous interactions where he knew that I loved him while he made his mistakes. When a child makes a mistake, he only needs to feel loved and to learn, not to apologize or feel guilty.

As my children became more certain that they were loved all the time, despite their mistakes, our conversations about accountability became easy and brief. Two years after the interaction above, we had another one about the garbage:

Me: "Joseph, I see the garbage wasn't taken out this morning."

Joseph: "You're right. I stayed up too late reading and watching television. This morning, I chose to get a few more minutes of sleep instead of doing my jobs around the house. I was selfish."

And then Joseph took out the garbage.

That is how we learned to handle mistakes in our family. It is so much easier, faster, and more effective than the old way which involved excuses, lies, anger, apologies, lectures, etc. Apologies accomplish little. What we really need is to see the truth about our mistakes, after which we *will* gradually make them less, without being punished and shamed. In addition, when we tell the truth and feel accepted, we feel loved and happy.

"You make me so mad."

We tell few lies more frequently than this one — often implied silently. We also use it in its indirect form: "He/she makes me angry."

The Truth

"You have the right to make your own choices and mistakes, but not when they inconvenience *me*. I'm angry that you have failed to recognize — even for a moment — that the world exists for the purpose of making *me* happy."

"Fine."

We commonly say this when people ask how we're doing. The question is rarely sincere, but is asked only as a social custom.

The Truth

1. "I feel unloved and alone all the time. I desperately want you to like me, and I'm afraid you won't if you see what I'm really like."

2. "I'm a terrible husband and father. My wife is obviously not happy to see me. My children avoid me and don't listen to me. I can't remember the last time one of them started a conversation with me. And I hate my job. Overall, I'm not happy with my life."

3. "I feel useless. My husband doesn't pay attention to me anymore. I'm losing any influence I ever had with my children. And I'm getting fat and feeling totally unattractive. I look at my life and wonder what went wrong."

Discussion

Most people don't really want to know how we're feeling. In those cases, an insincere "fine" is an appropriate response. However, we need to think about the real answer, and as we're learning to tell the truth about ourselves, we need to practice telling the truth with people who can accept and love us.

Silence

Silence is often a lie, a way of withholding what we know to be true.

The Truth

"Whenever I speak, I'm afraid that somebody will think I'm stupid and then criticize me or laugh at me. That's happened so many times in the past that now I stay quiet."

Discussion

Andrew (pp. 220-1) is an example of dishonest silence.

Laughter

Many of us laugh nervously when we're in situations that are uncomfortable for us.

The Truth

"When I'm with other people, I've learned that if I periodically smile or laugh as I talk, other people feel obligated to smile or laugh with me. That helps me to not feel as alone and exposed when I'm talking, and it also eliminates those moments of embarrassing silence that happen when I say something stupid."

Discussion

We can't tolerate the pain of looking stupid and being laughed at. If we laugh first, we know that people will tend to laugh *with* us instead of *at* us. But the truth works far better. When we simply say we're nervous as we speak, most people are understanding. And then we experience the enormous reward of an honest relationship with those people.

"This is frustrating."

The Truth

1. "This job is more demanding than I'm used to, and I'm afraid that if I fail, I'll look foolish in front of everybody."

2. "I'm angry that my boss gave me this assignment. He knew I couldn't do this, but he made me do it anyway. Sometimes I think he does this on purpose."

3. "I'm angry that you won't change who you are to make me happy."

Discussion

"Frustrated" is a word we use to disguise our fear and anger. But then we can't be seen clearly by those we talk to, and we suffer the ultimate penalty of feeling alone.

"I didn't mean to offend you."

Another variation on this is, "I'm not criticizing, but . . ."

The Truth

"I've been empty and afraid all my life, so I feel helpless and overwhelmed all the time. Criticizing people — including you — gives me an opportunity to express my anger and get a feeling of power. When

I make other people uncomfortable, I feel less helpless for a moment. I knew that what I said to you would probably hurt your feelings. It's something I've done many times before."

Discussion

We do things to hurt people more than we'd like to admit, and certainly more than we're aware of. When people hurt us, we feel helpless and weak. Hurting them gives us a feeling of power.

"I'm just not in love with her anymore."

The Truth

"I'm a completely selfish human being. When my partner doesn't give me everything I want and make me happy all the time, I have no more use for her. I don't love people. I use them."

Discussion

People commonly use "we're just not in love anymore" as an excuse to end a relationship. We want to be entertained and have someone to make us feel good constantly, and when that doesn't happen, we move on to a fresh source of Imitation Love.

"I forgot."

This is the answer we often give to a question about an assigned task we didn't accomplish.

The Truth

"I was doing the things I wanted to do, and that certainly didn't include what you wanted. I put that way down on my list of priorities and completely forgot about it."

Discussion

We don't forget to do the things we want to do. We don't just forget to eat. We don't forget what time our shift at work ends, or when our birthday is. We forget the things we don't want to do.

"Give Mommy a kiss."

Parents say things like this to their children all the time. "Tell Daddy you love him." "Give Mommy a hug before you go to bed."

The Truth

"I have felt lonely and unloved all my life. When you smile at me or kiss me, I feel less alone and more important. I need the affection I get from you, and to some extent, I can control it. I can't ask for love from adults as directly as I can from you."

Discussion

Although we hate seeing it, most of us expect our children to love us, and we prove that with our requests — often demands — for respect, obedience, courtesy, and affection. It's the responsibility of parents to love and teach children. We don't do it intentionally, but we place considerable responsibility on our children to make us feel good and look good. We make that clear every time we're disappointed in them and every time we say, "I'm angry because you ... " Children are not responsible for the feelings of their parents.

For much more on this subject see *The Truth About Parenting*.

Chapter 29

Exercises

We can learn how to tell the truth about ourselves, feel loved, and love others from the ordinary experiences of everyday life. However, we can significantly accelerate that process by participating in exercises designed to provide opportunities to be loved and love others.

These exercises can be done by any two or more people who are interested in learning and growing. Relative strangers tend to do these exercises quite effectively because they feel like they have little to lose with someone they don't know and may never see again. They are therefore more willing to take a risk and tell the truth about themselves. I suggest that two people who are having problems in a relationship *with each other* **not** do the exercises together. Without meaning to, they will tend to use the exercises as an opportunity to blame each other, rather than tell the truth about themselves.

Doing the exercises requires no special training. However, those who have read *The Truth About Relationships* will have a great deal more to talk about than most people who have not. The presence of a wise man during the exercises is most useful, but you'll discover that as you do them, you'll make wise men and women of yourselves.

Each exercise can be repeated many times. The more you learn, the more you'll get out of an exercise you've done before.

I will describe each exercise as though it were being done by two people. However, they can all be done by groups of any size.

Guidelines

I suggest several guidelines to be considered with these exercises:

1. There is one speaker and one listener. In groups, there is one speaker, while everyone else is a listener. That is the First Rule of Seeing, p. 108.

2. Read the whole exercise before starting it. It can be helpful to look in the "Comments" section of each exercise to learn from the experiences of other people who have done that exercise.

3. The listener does not offer comments while the speaker is talking. If the listener speaks while the speaker is expressing himself, the listener will be thinking about what he's going to say instead of really listening to the speaker.

4. After the speaker has finished, he becomes a listener and the listener becomes the new speaker. It's important that the new speaker not use this opportunity to comment on what the original speaker said.

5. After both participants (or everyone in a group) have had the opportunity to be the speaker, they talk about what they learned—mostly about themselves, but also what they learned about their partner. This part of the exercise is not a place for lecturing, arguing, debating, or contradicting what any speaker said. Many of the lessons that other people have learned during a particular exercise are described in the "Lessons" section of that exercise.

Additional Exercises

Additional exercises are found in *The Wise Man* and *The Truth About Parenting*. They provide even more opportunities for us to tell the truth about ourselves and be seen, accepted and loved.

Exercise #1
Telling the Truth About Ourselves

For 1-2 minutes, the first speaker tells the truth about himself and the listener listens without speaking. The listener then becomes the speaker and repeats the exercise. Both participants then talk about what they learned from speaking and from listening (see Lessons below).

Comment

When we hide the truth about ourselves, we feel alone and can't have loving relationships with anyone. Truth-telling creates the possibility of being seen, accepted, and loved. It's especially effective to talk about our mistakes and flaws. Obviously, it's hiding our imperfections — not hiding our successes — that keeps us feeling alone.

We have a tendency in this exercise — and elsewhere — to talk about *things* rather than ourselves. We talk about our jobs, our house, our children, etc. But if we want to feel seen and accepted, we must eventually share the truth about who *we* really are, warts and all. Following are some examples of telling the truth about ourselves:

"I feel stupid doing this exercise. It's embarrassing."
"I'm not as happy as I want to be. I guess that's why I'm here talking to you now."
"Not many people know that I take an anti-depressant. I've been doing that for over a year."
"I sometimes drink more than I should."
"I've been pretty selfish all my life. What **I** want has always been more important than what other people want."
"Telling you the truth makes me nervous, which must mean that I don't do it very much. I tend to hide who I really am from people."
"I've always been ashamed about how short I am."

"I have not been a loving husband. I yell at my wife and usually ignore
         what she wants."
"I feel alone and afraid most of the time."
"I worry a lot about what people think of me."
"I'm embarrassed about being overweight."

Lessons

1. "I felt afraid while I was telling you the truth about myself, but it got
easier the more I did it. And now I feel a big relief that I can really be
myself with someone and stop hiding."

2. "After I told you the truth about myself, I felt less alone."

3. "When you talked about yourself, I felt closer to you. It didn't
matter to me that you had done stupid things in your life. I care more
about you more now than I did before."

4. "I felt like you were really listening to me as I talked about myself,
and I liked that. I haven't had many experiences like that."

5. "I'm amazed at how much I've learned about you in these few
minutes. I know more about you than I do about most of my friends
that I've had for years."

6. "I'm learning how little anybody knows about me. You know more
about who I really am after two minutes than most people I've known
for years.

Exercise #2
Fear

For 1-2 minutes, the speaker tells the listener about his fears. The listener then becomes the speaker and talks about his fears. And then they both discuss what they learned (Lessons).

Comment

The more we tell the truth about ourselves, the more we create opportunities to be seen and accepted. We feel most loved when we feel accepted with the qualities we're ashamed of — like our fears. When we can talk about our fears and feel accepted, we lose our reason to be afraid.

Examples of fears:

"I've always been afraid that people would laugh at me and think I was stupid if they really got to know me. I'm afraid right now that you'll learn too much about me and not like me."
"I'm afraid of losing my job."
"I'm afraid that my marriage will never be better than it is, and I don't much like how it is now."
"When I was a kid, I never raised my hand to answer a question in class because I was afraid somebody would laugh at me. I'm still afraid to talk around people for the same reason."
"There are times when I drink to make my fears go away."
"I'm afraid my children don't love me."
"I'm afraid to admit that I don't know nearly as much as I always pretend that I do."
"I'm afraid to tell you what I'm really thinking, or you'll think I'm crazy."
"I'm afraid of dying."

Lessons

1. "What a relief that was! I've never talked about being afraid before."

2. "As you talked about your fears, I felt closer to you. And that helps me to believe that my own fears might not be disgusting to other people."

3. " After this, I think it will be easier to tell the truth about myself again."

4. "I felt accepted by you when I described my fears. I feel less anxious and alone right now."

5. "I never realized how afraid I am."

Exercise #3
Telling the Truth
About How I Get and Protect

For 1-2 minutes, the speaker describes his Getting and Protecting Behaviors to the listener. The listener then becomes the speaker. And then they discuss what they learned (Lessons).

Comments

The "bad" things we do are just behaviors intended to protect us and to get Imitation Love. This exercise requires more thinking than the truth-telling of Exercises 1 and 2. I therefore recommend two things before doing Exercise #3:

1. Review the principles found in Chapter 4.
2. If possible, have someone present who has experience with identifying Getting and Protecting Behaviors — a wise man.

Following are some examples of things the speaker might say:

"When someone criticizes me, I protect myself by **attacking** them, usually with anger. I've done that more times than I can count."

"I'm always afraid of making mistakes and being laughed at, so I tend to avoid people (**running**)."

"People tell me I complain a lot, and I'm beginning to see that's true. When I complain about how unfairly I've been treated, I get people to sympathize with me (acting like a **victim**)."

"I talk about the good things I do so that people will be impressed and like me. But of course I don't tell them I'm trying to get them to like, so that's **lying**."

"I hide my mistakes and blame them on other people (**lie**), because I'm afraid of looking bad."

"I get angry (**attack**) at my kids a lot, but that's not their fault. I just feel empty and afraid about things that have nothing to do with them."

Without interrupting the speaker excessively, it's occasionally helpful to encourage him to provide specific examples of the things he says. When he says he gets angry at people, ask him to give an example from the last couple of days. That allows him to feel even more seen and accepted.

Lessons

1. "I didn't realize until today how much I manipulate people to like me. And it doesn't work anyway. It only feels good for a short time, and what I get doesn't really make me feel loved or happy."

2. "As we talk, I'm realizing that when I protect myself, I always feel alone. Being truthful with you here has felt much better than protecting myself from you."

3. "As I listen to you talk about protecting yourself, I begin to see that when people are angry at me, they're not really trying to hurt me — they're just protecting themselves. That makes it stupid for me to get angry at them."

Chapter 30

Advanced Problem Solving

After publication of the first edition of *The Truth About Relationships*, I received thousands of questions from people all over the world asking for help with their specific problems. In this chapter, I'll use some of those questions to provide additional examples of how to implement the principles of the book to real-life situations. To avoid repetition to you, I will answer the questions with the assumption that the questioner has read the book.

I Hate My Job

"I've been working at this job for ten years, and I hate it more every day. I do the same old thing day after day, and it's never going to change. My boss never appreciates anything I do, either. I want to quit and do something else, but I'm not really qualified to do another job and the pay in this one is pretty good. And I have a family to support. My wife would go crazy if I took a job with a pay cut. As much as I hate working here, I don't see how I can quit. Between my job and my marriage, I'm getting depressed. What can I do?" (John from Portland, Maine)

Your real problem is not your job. If you were drowning, and a mosquito landed on the tip of your nose, which would be your most important problem, drowning or the mosquito? Easy question, right? So is yours. As annoying as your job certainly is all day, it's still a mosquito. Your real problem is the fact that you feel unloved, empty, and alone. And in that condition, nothing you do about your job will make you genuinely happy. If you used your last ounce of strength repeatedly swinging at the mosquito while you were drowning, would you be happy?

You need to address the emptiness in your life first, and then everything else will become easier to deal with. You need to learn to tell the truth about yourself and find people to love you. As you feel unconditionally loved, one of two things will happen:

1. You'll discover that you don't mind your job at all. When you find Real Love, your whole life changes. You become happy *without* changing your job. I've seen that happen many times.
OR
2. Feeling loved and happy, you'll see everything more clearly and will know what you want to change about your career. When we're empty and afraid, we can't see anything clearly. Every decision becomes hopelessly complicated.

It's a promise. As you feel more loved, one of those two things will happen. While you feel unloved, you're too miserable to be happy in any job. And you're too distracted to make a good decision about changing jobs. You probably don't do your best work in the job you're in now, either. Feeling unconditionally loved makes a huge difference in the way we feel and act in every aspect of our lives.

First Date

"I've heard you talk about the importance of telling the truth about ourselves in relationships. But I'm single, and many of my relationships are with men I'm dating. I can't imagine being truthful on a first date. If I told a guy everything about me as soon as we met, I'd scare him off and never see him again. So what do you recommend on a first date?" (Sandra, Vancouver, British Columbia)

We are unbelievably afraid of each other. We're terrified that if people see what we're really like, they won't like us. So what do we do? We put on a pretty face. We wear our best clothes. We're very careful to say the right things. We make ourselves look good in every possible way so that we'll create a favorable impression. It's an obsession with us, isn't it? We worry about it all the time. We read magazines for tips on the subject. We starve ourselves, throw up, and get plastic surgery to sculpt our bodies so people will think we look great. It seems there is nothing we won't do to make people think that we're worth liking.

Now some of that sounds like a good idea, doesn't it? Who wants to create a *bad* impression, after all? From the time we're babies, we've heard, "You only get one chance to make a good first impression." But let's say that you go out on a first date with some guy. And by saying and doing all the right things you succeed in convincing him that you're a great person. Now what? Now you have to *keep* doing all those things in order to continue earning his approval of you, don't you? That's a *lot* of work. And worst of all, after all that effort, he doesn't really like **you**. He likes the very best picture of you that you could paint. He likes a small part of you, and you have to work very hard to be sure that he never sees the *rest* of you. He doesn't know who you really are at all.

And what happens when the two of you spend more and more time together? Eventually, he *will* see the rest of you. There's no way you can hide all of you from him forever, especially if you actually get *married*, heaven forbid. And that's just what happens when people get married. They discover that this person who had sold them that great impression is not what they hoped. Both partners realize that they were swindled, even though it was not intentional. Everywhere we look, people are lying to each other, leading each other on, and trying to get everyone to think they're getting something better than what they're really getting. And then disappointment is inevitable.

How do we avoid all this? There's only one way. Tell the truth in the beginning. Right from the start. If you tell people who you are from the first word, how can you ever deceive or disappoint them? Impossible. Now it's true that if you're honest with men on the first date, there *will* be some who won't like you — who will, in your words, be scared off, never to be seen again. **So what?!**

Do you really want a relationship with a guy whose affection you have to *buy*? Do you really? Do you want a relationship with someone you have to keep lying to, that *will* someday be disappointed in you when he learns the truth about you?

You lose nothing by telling the truth in the beginning. You just find out *now* what you would learn in the end anyway. Would you rather learn that a man doesn't like you right now, after talking to him for five minutes — or in six months, after you've gotten your hopes up and invested your whole heart in him? Would you rather experience a brief let-down now or would you rather lead some man along and go through a divorce after ten years of marriage and three children? Is there really a question in your mind about that?

It's no contest. Telling the truth is the way to go. We keep telling our lies only because we've never seen it done any other way. We simply can't imagine what a completely honest relationship would look like. Let me tell you what it looks like. If you keep telling the truth on first dates and in other areas of your life, you'll eventually attract people who will accept and love you for who you really are. You will experience the unbelievable freedom of being yourself all the time — no lies, no pretending, no working to please people, no worrying that somebody might not like you. You'll know what it's like to have people care about *your* happiness without you doing anything to earn it. There's no feeling like it in the world.

It all starts with you telling the truth about yourself. So what do you say in the beginning, on that very first date, when you've never done this before? That can be a bit scary. Start with little things. Say this to your date:

"I get nervous on first dates because I want the guy I'm with to like me. In the past I've never admitted that out loud. Instead I've pretended that I was real calm and cool. But I've decided not to pretend anymore. I hate pretending."

That's not a complicated thing to say, and if you say it, two things will happen. First, your courage to tell the truth will grow. Second, you'll learn a lot about the guy you're with. If he looks at you like you just stepped out of a alien space ship, you're done with him. If he's not fascinated with your attempt to be honest, you can be almost certain that he doesn't want anything to do with the truth, and you don't want anything to do with him. Forget about him. But if he is interested in a genuinely truthful relationship, as some men are, he'll jump on a statement like that, and you two will have a great conversation. You might even have a great relationship.

Some other things you could say:

"I was going through my closet tonight to pick out something that looked good, but I decided to wear something comfortable instead. I don't like it when I try to impress people. It doesn't feel honest."

"I've lied to guys a lot in the past. I've pretended to like sports when I don't. I've acted like I was interested in their cars when I didn't really care about them. I think it's stupid now, but I wanted them to like me."

Always stick with the truth. It will attract the kind of man you really want. If you don't tell the truth, you won't like what you get. And you don't have to tell everything about yourself in the beginning. Just start with little things.

Help! I'm Shy

"I just don't feel comfortable around other people. Unfortunately, I'm in a business where occasionally I have to attend meetings and even parties where socializing is important. And I hate it. Some people are able to naturally talk about everything, and those people are popular with everybody in the room. That can be a real business advantage, and I feel myself losing out. And it's more than just business. Even in my personal life, I just don't know what to say to people, and that leaves me on the outside of a lot of conversations and relationships. I don't want to feel alone all the time. What can I do?" (Matthew, Galveston, Texas)

There's only one reason that we're shy around people and don't know what to say. We're *afraid* of people. We're afraid that when other people hear what we have to say, they'll change their minds from wondering if we're stupid and ridiculous to being absolutely certain of it. And if people think we're foolish, they won't like us. It always comes back to that, doesn't it? We're afraid that nobody will love us. So we stay to ourselves, afraid to take any risk that might make us unlovable.

The problem with that approach is that we end up constantly alone, the worst feeling of all. There's only one way out of this dilemma. We simply must learn to tell the truth about ourselves and create opportunities for people to unconditionally accept and love us. But we don't have to do that in the environments that frighten us most, like at work where our livelihood is at stake. We can start with casual friends, where the risk is less.

Most of us have so little experience with telling the truth about ourselves that we don't have the first clue about how to start. That's one reason I wrote *The Truth About Relationships*. Many people have told me that they began an honest relationship with a friend by simply saying, "I've been reading this book about relationships, and I'm learning some things. Would you be interested in reading it?" It's an easy and non-threatening way to find out which of your friends are interested in developing a deeper relationship. You have nothing to lose. If someone turns down your offer to read the book, you'll have the same relationship you had before. But if someone takes you up on your offer and begins to share the truth with you, you've gained a great deal.

Once you've experienced some real acceptance and unconditional love, you'll find that socializing with other people becomes much easier. It has to. As you feel loved, you become less afraid of *everyone*, and then you lose your reason to carefully watch what you say as you talk with people. I could explain this all day, but you'll never understand it fully until you actually experience it. Go for it. Learn to tell the truth about yourself and see how your life changes as you feel accepted and loved.

When we don't feel loved, we're afraid of everything. When we do feel loved, there's nothing to be afraid of.

All I Do Is Take Care of Kids

"I used to have a real life. And then I got married and had kids. Now my husband goes off to work every day, and I stay home all day long with an eighteen-month-old and a four-year-old for company. While other people are making business deals, having stimulating intellectual conversations with their peers over lunch, and solving the problems of the world, I'm changing diapers, wiping noses, reading stories, and stopping arguments about who gets to play with a toy. How am I supposed to find a challenge in all this and enjoy myself, instead of resenting the fact that everyone else is having a great time while I'm babysitting all day?" (Jennifer, Webster City, Iowa)

All the grand accomplishments of other people look so attractive, don't they? In my lifetime, I have personally known men and women who healed disease, sent rockets into space, analyzed the sub-atomic structure of matter, changed the course of rivers, and made policies that affected the lives of millions. As a surgeon, scientist, business-man, employer, lecturer, and author, I've done many of those things myself. And all those awe-inspiring activities count for nothing com-pared with loving a single human being. I mean that. All those worldly wonders mean *nothing* if people aren't happier as a result. What does it matter if we fly faster, see farther, dive deeper, know more, and live longer, if our souls are withered and wasted? I've also known some of those powerful and successful people as they've approached the end of their lives, and many would gladly have given all they had for the sensation of being unconditionally loved and genuinely happy. But they didn't have the slightest idea how to do that.

You have the opportunity as a wife and mother to do the greatest good in the world as you love your family. However, that is an impos-sible dream until you first feel loved yourself. Right now the idea of loving your children probably seems like just another burden that you can hardly stand to bear.

So do the one thing that you *can* do right now. Learn how to feel unconditionally loved yourself. Read The Truth About Relationships if you haven't. Re-read it if you have, and *do* the things you've read. Tell the truth about yourself and experience the unconditional love that is available to all of us. As you do that, you'll discover a happiness you never imagined. You'll find a fulfillment in changing diapers that most people will never know while designing rockets or merging corpora-tions. With Real Love, nothing else matters; without it, nothing else is enough.

My Son Is Using Drugs!

"I don't know what to do. My son is fifteen years old. He was always a delightful boy, the pride of my life. But in the last year or so, some-thing has happened to him. He doesn't do his homework. His grades have been slipping. He doesn't want to do anything with the rest of the family. He ignores his chores around the house. He seems to avoid me most of the time. And the other day when his mother was picking up some clothes off his floor to do the laundry, she found some marijuana in the pocket of his jeans. I can't believe it. What happened to the sweet kid that used to live here? How do I handle this? I don't want to yell at him or hit him like my own father used to do, but I'm afraid that if I do nothing, this will only get worse." (Mike, Klamath Falls, Oregon)

First, it's wonderful that you're concerned enough about your son to ask someone else for advice. That takes courage. Now let's look at what he's doing. Your son is being irresponsible and rebellious. He doesn't want to be with you. And now he's breaking the law. Rather than get worked up about how bad all that looks, or try to control his behavior, let's understand that all those behaviors are just symptoms of your son's real problem. *That* is what we need to address, not the symptoms.

If we put a perfectly healthy plant into the ground and then fail to water it, eventually it will begin to wilt and turn brown. Would it help to blame the plant? Of course not. Should we paint the leaves green so everything will look better? Ridiculous. The brown leaves and wilting stems are simply an indication that we need to water the plant, and when we do that, the plant will probably respond in a positive way.

And so it is with your son. When children need to be "watered," they tell us just as clearly as plants do, but they don't do it with brown leaves. They do it with anger, crying, violence, bad grades, rebellion, disobedience, alcohol, drugs, etc. And they don't need us to blame them or control their bad behaviors, which are just symptoms of the real problem. What children need more than anything else by far — as much as a plant needs water — is the feeling that they are unconditionally loved. Any child who exhibits the above behaviors is clearly telling us that he does *not* feel loved. And that is a *parent* problem.

Understandably, parents don't like hearing that. They feel like they're being told that they're bad parents, and that's not the case at all. I believe that parents love their children as well as they can. However, parents obviously can't give their children what they never got themselves. If we were not unconditionally loved ourselves, we can't offer that kind of love to our children.

The greatest gift that you can give your son right now is to admit that he does not feel unconditionally loved, and the most obvious person responsible for that is *you*. There is no blaming in that. It's just the way it is. For many years, I did the best I could as a father, but I did not love my children unconditionally. I *couldn't* have — I'd never seen unconditional love myself. So I praised my children and "loved" them when they were obedient, successful, grateful, and otherwise "good." But when they were "bad," I was disappointed, critical, and often angry. That kind of love is worthless to a child. As a result, my children felt empty, unloved, and miserable. They naturally reacted by using anger, rebellion, alcohol, drugs, and many other Getting and Protecting Behaviors.

I tried to get them to stop, but nothing worked until I finally admitted that they simply didn't feel loved, and that I was the reason they didn't. I essentially started my life all over. I learned to tell the truth about myself. I found people to accept and love me. I learned how to love from the beginning, like a child. As I shared that love with my children, all of their "bad" behaviors disappeared without me ever telling them to stop. When children feel loved, they don't need to do those things to deal with their pain.

I suggest the same course to you. It works. At first it's hard to admit that you're the problem when your children are unhappy, but it becomes obvious when you accept it, when you do something about it, and when you see the results of your efforts.

In the short term, I would suggest that you sit down with your son and tell him that you know about the marijuana, and that you love him no matter what he does. Then tell him that the reason he's using the marijuana is that something is missing in his life, and that you're the reason for that. Tell him that you're learning how to be a more loving father, and that as you get better at it, you hope he won't have a need in the future to be angry, or feel alone, or use drugs. Don't make him feel guilty. And don't give up.

My Husband Wants a Divorce

"I've been married for eight years. Two weeks ago my husband came to me and said he wanted a divorce. I think there's another woman involved, but he denies that. He says he's just tired of our marriage and wants to move on with his life. After spending my whole life on him and giving him three children, the coward actually said, 'I need my space.' I can't believe he could say that! What can I do to stop this from happening? Does he not understand what this will do to me and to the children?" (Sharon, San Diego, California)

A relationship is the natural result of people making independent choices. You only get to make your own choices, not his — even when his are inconsiderate, irresponsible, and destructive. That means that you don't get to "stop this from happening."

At this point, you don't know for certain that your husband will actually divorce you, but let's assume that he will and discuss what your choices are after that.

1. You can be bitter and angry at him for the rest of your life, which will guarantee that you'll be miserable until you're dead. It will also have a terrible effect on your children. Many people do that after a divorce. What a stupid decision.

OR

2. You can completely accept his decision and move on with making the rest of your life happy.

We spend so much time grieving our losses in the past and worrying about what bad things might happen in the future — all a waste of time. How much better it is to have faith that if we just do the best thing for us right now, we'll be happy. And the best thing is so simple. If we'll keep telling the truth about ourselves and create opportunities for people to accept and love us, we *will* feel loved. And then we'll learn to love others. That results in the greatest happiness imaginable. Why do we ever waste our time doing anything else?

If your husband decides to leave, let him go. Gladly. Then fill your life with the unconditional love that will always make you happy. When you have an abundance of Real Love and genuine happiness, you won't miss your ex-husband for a minute. That's a promise. I've seen it happen in the lives of many others.

My Boss Is a Monster

"I like my job. I've been in this line of work for twelve years and I want to keep doing it. But about a year ago, my supervisor was transferred here from another location. This guy is unbelievable. He doesn't think anything can get done unless he bullies and intimidates people. If anything goes wrong, he criticizes and yells at us like they we were children or idiots. I hate working with this guy, and so does everyone else. What can I do about this monster?" (Bill, Tampa, Florida)

Your supervisor is obviously an attacker, and people behave that way only when they're unloved, empty, and afraid. People who feel loved *never* have to act like that. Somewhere in his life, almost certainly early in childhood, he learned that he could make things happen by frightening people. All bullies learn that. Unfortunately, they also remain alone and miserable.

I can't tell you how many bullies I have watched melt into little puddles when they're loved. Love is what they want more than anything in the world, but they don't know how to ask for it. They don't even know they need it. But now you know what this man needs, and you can give it to him.

When your supervisor yells at people, what do they do? They pull away from him. They run, at least emotionally. And he feels them withdraw. He feels them silently label him as a monster. Although part of him enjoys frightening people, he doesn't like being labeled in that way, and he doesn't like feeling alone. He would prefer to be stroked like a puppy. Unfortunately, nobody dares to do that with this animal who always has his fangs bared.

You, however, can do just that. You understand that he's really just a frightened child who gets angry to protect himself. So the next time he comes into the room and yells at people, you can remember to picture him as a four-year-old who's throwing a tantrum. Would you run in fear from a four-year-old? I think not. Simply address what he needs — the specific task — without the slightest trace of fear, and then directly ask him if his needs have been met. Keep it up until he's gotten exactly what he wants, without any resistance.

He will almost certainly be stunned. As he sees that you're not afraid and that you don't run from him emotionally, he will feel less alone. He will feel seen and accepted by you. He may not know what to do with that at first, and you may not see an overwhelming change in his behavior immediately, but I have seen many monsters become pussy cats in short order. Bullies prefer to be feared over being ignored, but most of all, they want to be loved.

Chapter 31

Post-It Notes

Because most of us have little or no experience with Real Love, the principles in *The Truth About Relationships* may seem overwhelming at first. In this chapter, I suggest some simple aphorisms — mental "Post-It notes" — that can help us in everyday situations to make wiser choices than we have made in the past.

Real Love is caring about the happiness of another person.

When most of us say we "love" someone, we really mean that they make us feel good. Real Love is "I care about *your* happiness." Imitation Love is "I like how you make *me* feel."

With Real Love, nothing else matters; without it, nothing else is enough.

People who feel unconditionally loved have everything in life that matters. With Real Love, all other inconveniences become insignificant. And nothing else can ever make up for the lack of it.

When I'm unhappy in a relationship, the real problem is the lack of Real Love in my own life, not something my partner has done.

No one makes me angry.

We get angry to protect ourselves when we feel empty and afraid, and those feelings are caused by a lifetime of not feeling unconditionally loved. Our anger is not caused by something our partner does in a single moment.

All Imitation Love is worthless.

Praise, power, pleasure, and safety feel good for a moment, but no amount of Imitation Love can ever make us genuinely happy.

When I'm disappointed or angry, I'm selfish and wrong.

When we're disappointed or angry, we're concerned about *ourselves*, never the happiness of other people. We can never be unconditionally loving anyone in that condition. We get angry at people when they refuse to give up their right to make their own choices and do what **we** want instead — and we are always wrong to have such an expectation. Anger is selfish and destroys the possibility of loving relationships. Disappointment is just a milder form of anger.

When I do anything to get someone to like me, what I get is Imitation Love.

Every time we interact with another person, we need to ask ourselves whether we're doing anything at all to get that person to like us. If we do, what we get is paid for, not freely received, and therefore cannot be Real Love. There are two reliable signs that we're manipulating people: (1) we worry about what they think of us; and (2) we're disappointed when we don't get what we want.

A relationship is the natural result of people making independent choices.

Everyone has the right to make their own choices, even the choices we don't like. The moment we attempt to change someone, we don't have a real relationship with them. We can only be using them.

We only have three choices in a relationship: live with it and like it; live with it and hate it; or leave it.

In a relationship with another person, we can only make choices for ourselves. We do not have the right to make their choices for them.

Truth → Seen → Accepted → Loved

The process that leads to feeling loved starts with telling the truth about ourselves.

When I'm unhappy, I need to tell the truth about myself.

We're unhappy only because we feel unloved. The solution is therefore obvious: we need to tell the truth about ourselves to someone capable of accepting and loving us unconditionally. This is also the best response to the Getting and Protecting Behaviors of other people.

When I tell the truth about myself, I will find wise men and women to accept and love me.

Wise men and women are irresistibly drawn to the truth. As we tell the truth about ourselves, we attract wise men to us *and* we help to create them.

Faith is a decision I make to tell the truth even when I'm afraid of what might happen.

Our lives can't change until we simply decide to tell the truth about ourselves, even when we can't predict the results. We can't experience the benefits of being honest until we stop protecting ourselves and tell the truth instead.

When in doubt, tell the truth.

When all the other rules and guidelines about love and relationships slip your mind, remember this one: tell the truth about yourself and good things will happen.

No interaction is successful unless I feel loved or loving.

Love is the only thing that makes us happy. Why waste our time doing anything that doesn't contribute to real happiness? That may require changing some of our friends or surroundings.

Anything which interferes with feeling unconditionally loved or loving others is wrong.

All the moral ambiguities of the world dissolve in the face of understanding Real Love. When our goal is to unconditionally love other people, right and wrong become much easier to discern.

Disappointment and anger are incompatible with Real Love.

If we are disappointed or angry with others, we are not unconditionally loving them. If someone is disappointed or angry with us, that person is not unconditionally loving us.

I can always choose to be happy.

Telling the truth about ourselves and finding unconditional love is a choice we make. Since everything else leads to unhappiness, it's foolish to lie, be angry, run, and otherwise manipulate people. No matter what is going on around us, we can choose to feel loved, loving, and happy.

Shut up.

Until you feel more loved and loving, do not share your feelings with other people — *unless* the person you're talking to is a wise man or woman. In that case, they already feel loved and loving, and they can accept and love you while you're afraid, angry, and blaming.

One speaker

Remember the Rules of Seeing. When someone is talking, he (or she) is the speaker. Be quiet and let him speak. In that moment, he is the most important person in the world, and what he's saying is the most important subject. You can always speak later.

Mistakes are inevitable. It's a waste to feel guilty about my mistakes or angry about everyone else's.

Mistakes are unavoidable. That doesn't make them good, just inevitable. What we need when we make our mistakes is to see them, admit them, and feel loved. And then we *will* be less likely to make them the next time. We do not need to wallow in guilt about them. Nor do we need to punish other people for the mistakes that they make.

I get to make lots of mistakes.

Be grateful

When we feel unhappy, we're not remembering the infinite supply of unconditional love and joy that is available to us. Being grateful is simply seeing the truth about what we have.

There's no such thing as "unfair."

What is truly fair in life is that we all get to make our own choices and mistakes. As we do that, we unavoidably inconvenience each other. There's nothing unfair about that. Imagine a world where we had the power to make everything "fair" for ourselves. No one around us would have any freedom to choose, and that would be a miserable world indeed.

I never have the right to expect anyone to do something for me.

Expectations violate the Law of Choice. I have no right to expect someone to change who they are for my convenience: not when I want something badly; not when that person has the ability to give me what I want; and not even when they're married to me. Expectations are always selfish and destructive.

Do I want to be happy or right?

Insisting that our opinion is right — even if it is — has terrible consequences. We may win the argument, but we "enjoy" our victory alone and unhappy. Being right adds to the genuine happiness of no one.

If you want to stop an argument, admit that you're wrong.

It's easy. You can always find something you're wrong about. And again, do you want to be happy or right?

Everyone is lovable.

When we feel loved ourselves and see people clearly, we understand that all their "ugly" behaviors come from a lack of Real Love. Everyone needs to be loved and is worth loving.

We can't love other people until we first feel loved ourselves.

We can't give what we don't have. We first have to tell the truth about ourselves and feel unconditionally loved, *and then* loving others is natural and effortless.

Index

Index

Attacking:
　　examples, 36, 37-8, 42, 46,
　　　　51, 88
　　Getting and Protecting
　　　　Behavior, 36
　　responding to, 223-4, 278-9
"Bad, "we're not when we hurt
　　other people, 40
Bad behaviors:
　　all caused by lack of Real
　　　　Love, 85
　　defined, 24-5
Becky, 224
Benjamin, 148-9, 188-9
Beth, 222-3
Bill, 191-2
Birthday present, 167
Blaming:
　　ineffective, 8
　　understandable, 5
Blindness:
　　causes expectations, intoler-
　　　　ance, and being alone,
　　　　135-6
　　eliminating with Real Love,
　　　　136, 153
　　when empty, afraid, and an-
　　　　gry, 43, 111
Brain tumor, 115-6
Brenda, 175-6
Bruce, 170-2, 182-3
Bullies, 278-9
Business:
　　contracts, 190
　　Real Love in, 190-1
But, 24

Cabin, 237-8
Carl, 213-7
Carol, 95-7
Charles, 154-5
Charlotte, 102-5
Cheryl, 18-9
Choice (and choosing):
　　everything we feel and do is,
　　　　55
　　Law of, 55
　　like strokes in a painting, 55
　　make the best we can see, 85-
　　　　6
　　make ours but not those of
　　　　others, 57
　　must make our own, 55, 212-
　　　　3
　　nothing more important, 55
　　see Relationships, choices in
Chris, 87-91
Christopher, 5-6
Chuck, 32-3
Clinging:
　　examples, 38, 52
　　Getting Behavior, 38
　　sign of need, not love, 48-9
Commandments, list of Getting
　　and Protecting to avoid, 199
Conditional love:
　　defined, 17
　　emptiness of, 17
　　examples, 23
　　vs. Imitation Love, 33
　　vs. Real Love, 23
Conflict: